A Galloper at Ypres

A Galloper at Ypres

The Personal Experiences of a British Army
Aide-de-Camp at the First and Second Battles of
Ypres during the First World War

Patrick Butler

LEONAUR

A Galloper at Ypres
The Personal Experiences of a British Army Aide-de-Camp at the First and Second Battles of Ypres during the First World War
by Patrick Butler

First published under the title
A Galloper at Ypres

Leonaur is an imprint of Oakpast Ltd

Copyright in this form © 2019 Oakpast Ltd

ISBN: 978-1-78282-824-2 (hardcover)
ISBN: 978-1-78282-825-9 (softcover)

http://www.leonaur.com

Publisher's Notes

Contents

TO
MY MOTHER

HUIZE BEUKENHORST, ZILLEBEKE.

For long the Headquarters of the Seventh Division during the First Battle of Ypres.

CHAPTER 1

Before Going Out

At 4 o'clock on the afternoon of Sunday, 4th October, 1914, I was sitting in the garden of the Grand Hotel, Lyndhurst—a beautiful day of sunshine—when I heard my name called by the general. He told me to get ready at once to accompany him in the motor to the War Office. I had only time to run up to my tent about a quarter of a mile away and seize my greatcoat, sword, and a haversack into which I hastily stuffed a few articles. On my way there H——, one of my brother staff officers, told me that our orders for embarkation had come. My mother, who had come over from Ireland to spend the last few days with me, and to whom I had whispered the news, met me on my way down from my tent and helped me to carry some of my things. She and I had all along known that when the summons came it would be sudden, but in such matters the actual happening always takes one by surprise and this occasion was certainly no exception. For all we knew it was to be our final parting, and it was a very brief one. In an instant the general and I were on the Winchester road speeding towards London.

Two months before, almost to a day, the outbreak of war had found me stationed at the Regimental Depot in the quiet old Irish town of Clonmel. I had been posted there from India two years previously for a tour of duty. When, at the end of July, war had become a certainty, we Regular officers, attached to Special Reserve units, were told off for various not very exciting, but still necessary, jobs at home; and it looked as though considerable time might elapse before we should be able to get out with a battalion to the Front. My own battalion was still in India, and the post which was allotted to me a few days before mobilisation was that of Assistant Embarkation Officer at Rosslare, in the South of Ireland!

This post I took up at once, but before doing so I wrote to General C—— in London asking him to take me on his staff as Galloper. I had acted in this capacity to him on two occasions on manoeuvres. He had replied that he himself had no job, either abroad or at home, but that we should certainly all get out to the Front before long. During the few days I was at Rosslare the Reservists of our 2nd Battalion had passed through on their way to join the battalion at Devonport, and with them, among other officers, was my brother M——. After his boat had departed into the moonlight of that wonderful August night I went and sent off a telegram to the Secretary of the War Office, asking to be allowed to accompany the 2nd Battalion of my regiment to France.

Before morning the reply arrived:

Reference your wire accompanying 2nd Royal Irish to France stop you cannot.

This telegram caused us much discussion in our little mess at the end of the Rosslare pier. "Stop," to mean full stop, had been discarded several years, and the order had been that the symbol A A A was invariably to be used instead. So, this telegram might have meant:

You cannot stop.

We came to the conclusion, however, that the word had been used in its old sense, as indicating a full stop, for instead of receiving orders for the Front I was transferred to Dublin to perform the thankless duties of R.T.O. at one of the termini. By the 20th, all the important traffic connected with mobilisation had ceased, and I was ordered to join my Reserve battalion in Dublin. I had not long to endure that, but was ordered to proceed to Waterville, Co. Kerry, to take in hand a detachment that was guarding the cable station there, and that had been giving some trouble. Thus, I seemed to be further than ever from getting out to the Front, and the prospect of waiting at such work as this until the Reserve battalion was ready to go out was not alluring. I fired off another letter to General C——, and started for Waterville.

My first afternoon's journey only took me as far as Killarney, where I decided to spend the night. I went to an hotel which was full of German waiters (they said they were Swiss) and little besides. The next day I got to Waterville, at about 3 p.m., travelling from Cahirciveen to my destination in a motorbus, together with my servant, Weekes.

I had hardly been at Waterville an hour when a telegram was

handed me. It was from General C——, and was to say that he had applied for me as his *A.D.C.*, and that I was to come to London as soon as possible. Thus, in my harangue to the men of the detachment, which took place shortly afterwards, I was able to tell them that I had got my orders for the Front, and that if they did not mend their ways they would never be sent there, and when I dismissed them, they gave me three hearty cheers. F—— was in command of the detachment, and greatly envied me my good fortune.

In all my service I have always interpreted the phrase "as soon as possible" a good deal too literally. Quite probably the first occasion of my not doing so would have resulted disastrously—such is often the contrariness of human affairs, but the fact remains that having fulfilled the order literally and fetched up breathlessly at the ordained spot, I have always found that my haste has been unnecessary.

But this was war, and I was determined to leave nothing to chance. There was no train to Cahirciveen until the following morning. Someone at the Butler Arms Hotel, Waterville, told me that a man in the village had a motorcar for hire, and that most probably he would charge me nothing if I gave him a "chit" on the R.A.C., to which institution he was affiliated. I interviewed my friend, who readily assented to my proposal, and after swallowing a hasty dinner I set off for Killarney, a distance of some forty miles. There I knew I could catch the Cork-Dublin Mail early the following morning.

So, it came about that I and the faithful, silent Weekes once more took the road. We went by the way we had come, towards Cahirciveen, and very soon had to light our head-lamps, for the night came on pitch dark. During the last part of this twelve-mile run over an indifferent road I could see the glimmer of many lights far across the black water to our left. I knew that they marked the position of Valentia, and I told my driver that in Valentia I had a brother stationed and that it seemed strange to be passing so close to him at such a time as this and not to be able to see him.

"Why wouldn't you?" he cried. "I can run you down to the ferry as easy as easy and wait for you until you come back."

I assented, and soon we were drawn up beside a little public-house that formed the nucleus of the few houses of the ferry station. A big, burly, slightly inebriated longshoreman came out of the public-house, followed submissively by a much younger man. The big man introduced himself to me as the ferryman, and I think that I gathered that he doubled the part with that of acting harbour master. He expressed his willingness to put me across, and declared that he could do it in twenty minutes. There was a big sea running, and every now and then as we made the journey, I thought of divesting myself of my heavy military overcoat in case we should be swamped. But there was really no cause for alarm. The harbour master, garrulous and consequential to a degree, was nevertheless a past master of the art of managing a boat. From time to time there would be a word to the younger man, who was pulling in the bows, and the heavy boat would swing broadside on to the rollers and negotiate them beautifully. There were frequent directions to the young man not to lean too heavily on his oar, as it was "sprung," and I could see that he lived in mortal dread of the harbour master, whom he invariably addressed as "Sir."

In about half an hour we were across. It was but a few yards from the landing-stage to the little hotel, and there I learned to my disappointment that my brother had obtained a few hours' leave and was spending the night with friends about half-way to Killarney, along the road which I should have to take. After a drink with the young officers who were in the sitting-room, and amid wishes of God-speed, I left the hotel and recrossed in the ferry to the mainland. I found my servant (who was fully armed and looking very fierce) and the driver the centre of an admiring crowd of loafers, and very soon we had turned the car eastwards and were speeding towards Killarney.

For mile after mile our route lay along the edge of a large inlet. Just above us on our right ran the railway by which we had come that morning, with the towering cliff above it again, and on our left another cliff went sheer down to the sea. We had one considerable delay caused by a punctured tyre, but in course of time we reached the house where my brother was spending the night. By now it was nearly eleven, and the house was dark and still. I left the car at the gate, and went along the drive to the front door. Very soon both my brother and his host were down. We made a quaint little party around the dining-room table, and there, in that remote spot, we talked of many things.

The host's whisky was excellent, and I remember we repeated whole passages of a patriotic nature from Shakespeare. My host quoted Macaulay. *The Armada* was fetched from the bookshelf, and we read it through with appropriate emphasis. I felt amply justified in being elated. Was I not off to the biggest war there had ever been? But it was rather a sad farewell we bade one another, the brother and I, upon the doorstep. The remainder of that night's journey was uneventful, save that we some difficulty in obtaining a lodging in Killarney. Early next morning, the 27th August, I said goodbye to my excellent driver, and caught the mail train for Dublin. But from Limerick Junction I went round by Clonmel in order to pick up some kit. I caught the afternoon mail *via* Thurles and travelled up in the company of Lord Granard; who had just been appointed colonel of one of our new battalions. At Ballybrophy, on the way, I was joined by my eldest sister, and together we journeyed to Dublin. There my mother and eldest brother joined us, coming on from Kingsbridge by train to Amiens Street. At Westland Row the sister too, left. These war-time partings are trying.

Crossing from Kingstown to Holyhead the passengers were thrown into a state of great excitement by the sight of a long row of ships lights extending seemingly right across the Channel. Word was passed that it was portion of the Grand Fleet, but I knew that this could not be the case as the fleet in war time would not be so lit up. It turned out to be the herring fleet, pursuing its peaceful vocation.

Very early the next morning, 28th August, I arrived in London, and having proceeded direct to Portland Place I found that it was quite impossible to obtain admission to the general's flat. After a long delay I succeeded in routing a porter out of the back premises, and at about 7.30 I was shown into the general's bedroom and found him just being called. As soon as his man had retired, he told me the nature of his new appointment, which was to be kept very secret. He had been given the command of the 7th Division, which was about to be formed out of troops brought back from India, the Mediterranean and South Africa.

As originally constituted the British Expeditionary Force consisted, as is well known, of six divisions of infantry and one of cavalry, but it had soon become evident that this was not enough for the work before it. True, the 6th Division had not sailed at the time the 7th was formed, and it did not sail until well on in September, but the need of a 7th, 8th and 9th was quite apparent. General C—— was to command the 7th, which was to assemble at Southampton from the 31st August onwards. Until that date there was little for me to do, and so even this time my haste in coming over turned out to be unnecessary.

On the 31st August the general and I travelled down together to Southampton, and from that day the real hard work began. We established our headquarters at the Polygon Hotel, where we were very comfortable, making use of the large music-room for our deliberations and conferences. I had to pay several visits to London, chiefly on business connected with the purchase of mess stores, for to me as *A.D.C.* had fallen the task of arranging our feeding for the ensuing campaign.

During the few days we remained at the Polygon—from 31st August till 10th September—we received our chargers, and I found myself the possessor of three very fine Irish hunters. They had been chosen for their speed, and though later on I found that one of them required a good deal of urging to make him extend himself, I had no reason to be dissatisfied when I tried them. On 6th September the general had to go on a tour of inspection of various bodies of Territorials, and he did not rejoin headquarters until sometime after we had established them at Lyndhurst, in the New Forest. We went there on the 10th, and the work of preparation then began in earnest.

Long marches and field days took place daily, with conferences in the hotel ball-room after dinner each evening. About the 16th September my mother arrived from Ireland—a most sporting undertaking on her part, and an inexpressible joy to both of us to be together during those last few days. She had ample opportunities for studying a war division coming into being, and amply availed herself of them. She also painted the portraits of my three chargers, "Sportsman," "Dawn" and "Brightness." (My mother, Lady Butler, is the painter of "The Roll Call," "Scotland for Ever," "Quatre Bras," etc.—Author.)

On Sunday, the 20th, I walked with her to the spot behind the Scots Guards' Camp, where Father Bernard Vaughan was to say Mass in the open. It was a most impressive service. The sun shone brilliantly, and the thick golden bracken and background of forest trees made a beautiful setting to the scene. There was just enough breeze blowing to threaten to extinguish the two altar candles, so two stalwart privates of the Guards knelt one on either side of the altar and sheltered with raised hands the tiny flames.

About that time Tom Condon, a young Irishman who had looked after a couple of hunters for me during two seasons in Ireland, and for whom I had a great regard, came to join me as my groom. Tom belonged to a class which, alas! gives too few soldiers to the army—that of the prosperous small tradesman or farmer. His father kept a livery stable in Clonmel, and Tom had received from the Christian Brothers a very good education.

Under the terms of a special Army Order a certain number of better class young men were enlisted in the A.S.C. as grooms, cooks and chauffeurs. They were well paid, receiving four shillings a day pay, separation allowance if married, at the rate of 1s. 2d. a day, with 2d a day for each child, and a gratuity at the end of the war of £5.

They enlisted for the duration of the war only. Tom joined as one of these, and I was very pleased to have him. He took to the work like a duck to water, and thoroughly enjoyed it. He and my servant, Weekes, were the only two Irishmen in the Headquarters Camp besides myself. They had been friends at Clonmel and were now very glad of one another's company.

The days at Lyndhurst passed rapidly enough. The field days were of supreme value in getting our brigades and regiments, drawn from so many widely-separated countries, to work together. The forest was looking its best, whether in the real leafy portion or in those bracken-covered tracts that go by the name of "open forest." Often when I got an afternoon to myself, I would go for a ride in that beautiful country. One ride that I remember particularly was to Beaulieu, whither I hacked to leave the general's card on Lord Montagu, who had called on him. The general had remarked to me on his return from his tour of inspection that he had seen and appreciated more of rural England in that hurried tour than ever in his life before, so greatly did the possibility of losing it all for ever enhance its appeal. He was right, and we all felt the same. I think he almost foresaw the slaughter of our splendid division. Once he said to me at Lyndhurst: "Horrible to think of the holes that must be blown in them!" as we watched regiment after regiment defile past us on the road.

I have said what a very great joy it was to me to have my mother with me during those last ten days. Nobody could have been more appreciative of all that she saw. Little did those sunburnt men know, as they swung past, that the lady in black, who never seemed tired of watching them, was the artist whose pictures had brought home to thousands the pathos and glory of the soldier's calling. Lyndhurst village is a most charming little old-fashioned place, quite unspoilt. As evening fell, we would wander, she and I, up the street and away to some by-lane where we could talk uninterruptedly. I remember one such evening particularly. The warm afterglow of autumn was fast fading, and a pure moon, very serene, floated above the forest trees and the red-tiled roofs of the cottages. Soldiers going for an evening stroll would pass us, but we were safe from any vulgar curiosity on their part, for is not the relationship between mother and son the dearest theme of the soldier?

And so, this brings me back to where I started, within a day or so—to the Sunday afternoon, 4th October, when my general and I received our summons to London.

MAJOR-GEN. SIR THOMPSON CAPPER, D.S.O.,
COMMANDING 7TH DIVISION.

My General

CHAPTER 2

With the Seventh Division to Bruges

I have said that for all I or my mother knew that hurried farewell as I followed my general into the motor was to be our last, but as a matter of fact the instructions which he got in London from Lord Kitchener admitted of our travelling back by motor that same night to Lyndhurst, having about three hours' sleep in the hotel (in my case on the floor), and seeing our respective relatives for half-an-hour in the morning, between half-past seven and eight. My mother was down to give me my breakfast. The horses had already gone on, and some of the regiments were on the road. Very soon the staff had to follow. It was goodbye indeed.

How one dreads the "sadness of farewell"! It was a relief when the general rapped on the window of the car to me to stop, that he might curse a subaltern who was marching a section of guns to the station, and whose march-discipline was bad!

Arrived at the docks we had about three hours of frenzied work. We were told that Divisional Headquarters would go in the third ship, the *Armenian*, and accordingly we went on board and started to settle down. I began to try to collect the various component parts of the mess—cooks, food-baskets, etc., and to search in the bowels of the ship for my servant, groom and horses. Only accommodation, not food, was to be provided for us, and very elementary at that. The original order had been, I think, that the men were to take six days' rations with them; but at the last moment this was reduced to two, so that when we landed at our eventual destination (which was kept a profound secret) we found ourselves dependent for food upon the Belgian authorities.

I went below to look for my belongings. The dim and stuffy *vistas* swarmed with men, and down both sides the horses were jammed in long, uneasy rows. This was the lowest deck of all. Just above it there were more men, and a sort of loose boxes in which were tied the huge, heavy-draught horses allotted to our transport. One of these poor animals was behaving like a mad thing, and threatened to smash his way out of his pen, secured by the head as he was, by sheer weight and violence. Every now and then he would rear aloft, and get a leg over the side of the box in a sort of paroxysm of fear and rage. Poor brute! There was a crowd of men round him, and at first, I could not see what was taking place; but soon I heard the drip, drip of blood, and a trickle began to make its way through the planks on to the deck below, close to the companion at the foot of which I was standing. The sight was not pleasant.

After an interminable delay the cooks, groom and servant all reported to me, and I located my three chargers. As I escaped up to the light and air, I had to pass again near the monster draught-horse. I could see his huge bulk filling the stall, but he seemed strangely quiet now. I noticed that the men still crowded round, but they were more intent and reassured, and with a sort of curiosity in their faces. There were horror and pity in their looks, not cruelty. The drip, drip was now a steady outpouring of blood. It flooded the deck. They were bleeding him to death, a man told me. He had already staggered once, and would fall now at any moment. As I gained the deck, I fancied I heard the thud. The "merciful bullet" was impracticable here, on account of the congested state of the decks. Poor beast, his troubles were over early.

As soon as I appeared on deck and reported to the general he sent me to the far end of the docks to dispatch a telegram to Capitaine de B——, our *Officier de Liaison*, who was in London, telling him when to join us. Hardly had I done so when a breathless messenger arrived at the telegraph office to tell me that the general had altered his mind about the ship and decided to travel in the one that was to sail first, the *Minneapolis*. She was to sail at noon, and it was already nearly twenty minutes to. I was able to borrow a motor, and had perforce to ignore the owner's request that it might be sent back for him at once, or otherwise the transference of mess stores from one ship to another could not have been carried out.

Never shall I forget my feelings as I waited for one, at least, of my cooks to turn up and help me to get the mess stuff out of the pantry of the *Armenian*, where it had all been stacked. The minutes passed, and neither the cooks nor the messengers I had sent to look for them returned. At last in despair I borrowed some Coldstream privates, and was in the act of having the hamper, *degchies*, etc., passed down the very steep gangway on to the quay when both cooks appeared. We all stumbled down the gangway and hurried to where I had left the motor. Luckily it had not gone. There were five minutes left in which to get the outfit on board the new ship. The motor sprang forward, cooks and helpers bulging out of the doors and hanging on to the steps. Coming round a bend we met the unfortunate owner, D——, of the Coldstreams, who, in despair at not finding his car, had walked.

At the foot of the gangway I found the general. "Come on," he cried, "I want the general staff to come on board with me on this ship. We'll save about twenty hours. I can't think what they mean by telling us off to a later ship!"

The baskets and *degchies* were pushed and hauled on deck, and we followed. In a few moments we were off, leaving a protesting naval embarkation officer on the quay. I was sorry to have missed the encounter between him and my general.

The drawing-room above the saloon was reserved for the Divisional Headquarters Staff, and there, while the general and his two senior staff officers wrote orders, I helped D—— to sort maps. A complete new set had had to be issued to us at the last moment, the first lot having been the same as those issued to the rest of the Expeditionary Force, and therefore unsuitable. D—— told me confidentially that we were bound for Zeebrugge, in Belgium.

My two cooks turned out trumps, and we did very well with regard to meals. But had I not bundled the basket of stores on board at the last moment we should have had nothing to eat at all. We had the Northumberland Hussars (our divisional cavalry) on board, and other details. The Administrative Staff was left to follow in the *Armenian*.

We did not get to the Belgian coast without incident, and had we only known it we had little reason for feeling as secure as we did. It was said afterwards that a German submarine had been loose in the Channel, but all we knew at the time was that in the middle of the night we found ourselves in Dover harbour, with the searchlights playing on us, and another of our transports close astern. A short distance away on our starboard bow was a destroyer—part of our escort.

At about seven in the morning, Tuesday, 6th October, we arrived off Zeebrugge. None of the men, and not many of the officers, knew what land it was that lay ahead of us. The buildings of the little town were plainly visible, and away to the north we could see that island of ominous memory, Walcheren. Through my glasses I could see that the British and Belgian flags which were flying over the tallest buildings in Zeebrugge were at half-mast, and I feared from this that Antwerp must have fallen.

As a matter of fact, Antwerp did not fall until some days after we had landed. But I knew quite well at the time that it was *in extremis*, for I had heard on the best authority in London that it could not hope to withstand a serious assault. "A serious assault" was the very phrase used, and yet at the time of my being told this our newspapers were gravely informing the public that the place could hold out indefinitely. It reminded me of the earlier, but similar, case of Namur. I shall never forget seeing the announcement of its fall placarded in the streets of Dublin, when that morning's paper had stated that it would hold out for four months!

There was one ship in in front of us, already tied up to the splendid mole, and very soon the third of our little convoy came in too. That was all we were to have that day. These three ships brought General L——— and his Headquarters and the Queen's and Yorkshire Regiments. In every case a ship carried the halves of two battalions—Headquarters and half a battalion in one, together with half a battalion of another regiment, and the other half battalion, together with Headquarters and the other half of another regiment, in the other. This arrangement was caused by the fear of mines and submarines, to limit the liability of an entire unit being lost. Two halves could be more easily spared than one whole.

What a target for a raiding squadron did we not present! There we were at the end of a very long mole, utterly exposed from the sea, and with our men and horses crowding all the available quay-space. How well our naval blockade of the German coast told on this ticklish occasion! The problem, too, of rations for our men was becoming acute. Something of a miscalculation had been made, and we were faced with a serious shortage. But the Belgian authorities were very good. They could not do enough for us. Ten thousand rations would be handed over to us at once, they declared, while at Bruges and Ostend they had collected enough hay and oats to allow seven kilos of hay and six of oats to each horse *per diem*. This was an extremely timely and liberal offer, and though the full Belgian human ration was only equal to our half-ration, we had every reason to feel grateful.

Here I may as well give the composition of our division:—

Infantry: 20th, 21st, and 22nd Brigades.

20th Brigade consisted of: 1st Grenadier and 2nd Scots Guards, 2nd Gordon Highlanders, and 2nd Border Regiment.

21st consisted of: 2nd Wilts, 2nd Bedfords, 2nd Scots Fusiliers, and 2nd Yorkshire Regiment.

22nd consisted of: 2nd Warwicks, 1st South Staffords, 1st Royal Welsh Fusiliers, and 2nd Queen's.

14th Brigade R.H.A.

22nd and 35th Brigades R.F.A.

111th and 112th Heavy Batteries R.G.A.

54th and 55th Field Companies R.E.

21st, 22nd and 23rd Field Ambulances.

7th Signal Company R.E.

Divisional Cavalry: Northumberland Hussars (Yeomanry).

7th Cyclist Company.

This division was spoken of by men competent to judge as one of the finest that had ever left the shores of Britain. And so, it was! Seasoned men all. India and South Africa, and Gib., and Malta, and Khartoum had known them. What troops! What men to serve with!

After a tedious morning on the quay, at about 3 o'clock in the afternoon of the 6th, when most of the troops were under way to Bruges by road or by train, we of the Headquarters group took train ourselves.

What memories began to rise before me! Seventeen years before I had come to Bruges (but *via* Ostend that time) as a schoolboy, to spend a week or ten days there. The wonderful charm of the old city had left an ineffaceable impression on my mind, and to return to it now, in those strange, incalculable circumstances, was like revisiting impossibly in a dream some cherished haunt of childhood.

A Belgian officer of high rank had met us on arrival, and I find in the little notebook which I kept at the time the following:

Ghent, 2,000 men (Belgian infantry). Three regiments of cavalry. Auto machine gun reconnaissances. Staff will send instructions to G.O.C. from Anvers. Either send instructions here, or to Bruges.

As far as I could judge, we were supposed, at that time, to be under

21

the orders of the Belgian General Staff; and it was only later, when we had got to Bruges, that we heard of the Fourth Army Corps.

This was supposed to consist of our division and the 8th, which latter had been collecting and training near Winchester at the time of our leaving Lyndhurst, but was unable to leave England in time to be of any assistance to us.

On the evening of the 6th October, therefore, we of the Headquarters, and such troops as had already landed (about a brigade and a half), arrived in Bruges. All the way along in the train, from Zeebrugge to Bruges (about eight miles, though longer by road) the people turned out and cheered us wildly. What a difference such a reception makes in war! We all felt heroes, and the men simply revelled in the new sensation, so unlike anything which they had experienced at home.

We were cheered enthusiastically all along the route—from where we passed beneath the tall building over which I had spied the half-masted flags, and where there was a pathetic crowd of refugees in all conditions of life, to where we emerged from the railway station in Bruges itself. We passed to our carriages through the dense crowd before the entrance, and drove to the Hotel de Flandre, where we fixed our headquarters.

As soon as I could get away, I slipped out into the streets to see again the beautiful old town. It was an unforgettable scene. Bruges the quaint, the quiet, the sleepy, resounding to the cheers of a populace swollen by refugees from all over Belgium—cheers that were given back with interest by British troops as they marched and counter-marched through the city. "*Voici les Anglais!*" the cry would go up some side-street, and immediately with loud shouts and clatterings a new crowd would come to swell the solid rows of people who formed a triumphal avenue for our men. I saw again the belfry and that wonderful Chapel of the Sacred Blood. In an angle of the latter hundreds of women were kneeling on the rough cobble-stones, praying. A pale moon looked down upon the alternation of silver and shadow and glinted on the arms of the soldiers. Alas, that we were soon to leave the glorious old town to the mercies of the Germans!

I had a strange experience that night. I am not a sleep-walker, nor had I dined either late or heavily, but about two in the morning I suddenly found myself wide awake from a deep sleep and hanging out of my bedroom window! I fancied that I had awakened with a shout. A sort of unreasoning, uncanny terror was upon me, and I felt that whatever happened I must not look back into the room. Not until I had read the word "*Flandre*" on a swinging sign outside, and just below me, did I remember where I was, or realise how near I had come to falling on to the pavement beneath. In a few moments I was myself again and back in bed.

A curious thing about this incident was that an almost precisely similar one had occurred to me many years before. It was in the Constable's Tower of Dover Castle, at the time of my return from this very place, Bruges. I was sleeping in a little room in the oldest portion of the Tower, when I awoke quite suddenly and felt a sort of nameless dread which forced me to cram my face against the window *and remain looking out*. How well I remember the moonlight flooding the high walls of the castle opposite! After a while the terror died, and I was able to return to bed. Save that in the second case I did not awaken until I was hanging half out of the window, while in the former I woke in bed and was at the closed window in a flash, the two cases were exactly parallel, and the feeling of terror identical.

I dislike dwelling upon dreams, and have never attached importance to them. But these two cases were curious.

We spent the whole of the 7th October at Bruges. As our three brigades grew to their full strength they assembled in groups behind their outposts, at St. André, Oostcamp, Assebroucke, and Ste. Croix. I had to visit 22nd Brigade Headquarters at Oostcamp during the day and found them comfortably installed in an inn, the sentry outside being the centre of an admiring crowd. I was in a motorcar with a Belgian soldier acting as guide, and on our return, we made a detour to see the Lac d'Amour, which was looking very beautiful, with the clear outline of the spire of Notre Dame reflected in its waters. I also went with Sir Frederick Ponsonby to visit the churches and to admire again after all those years the tomb of Charles the Bold, with its quaint, brave old Burgundian motto, "*Je lay empris bien en aviengue.*"

I forget whether it was that night or the night before, but I think that night, that a smart little Frenchman in uniform came to our hotel and asked some of us to join him in a *petit verre*, (little glass). He was the Duc de Morny, and introduced to us by our liaison officer, who had caught us up. De Morny was straight from Antwerp, which was now at its last gasp. He told us much about the fighting there, and said that Colonel Seely had given the most extraordinary example of gallantry. He had, it appeared, saved a Belgian battery by rushing out in front of it among the German shells, just as the gunners had commenced to quit their pieces, and by his words and example had managed to restore their confidence to such an extent that they returned to their guns.

"Shells!" Seely kept shouting in French, "they don't hurt anybody!" We had the impression that we were in a precarious position at Bruges, but we did not think that we should be told to retire from there. Rather, it seemed that we should be ordered to take up as good a defensive position as possible, and when reinforcements had arrived be pushed up towards Antwerp. I was therefore looking forward to a night's rest on that 8th October, and I turned in fairly early. But I was hurriedly awakened in the middle of the night by D——, who said, "We're to move!" So, I got up and packed my kit and then went down to the general's office, where I found him poring over a map and dictating orders.

Chapter 3

Towards Antwerp

Orders had come from General Rawlinson to retire on Ostend, and the move was to start at daybreak. I had met the Duke of Westminster in the street the evening before, and both his chief and his chief's young brother had been at our hotel for a few minutes, but no orders had then been given for a retirement. Young R——— had distinguished himself by discharging at a house opposite a light quick-firing gun which was mounted on one of the Naval Brigade armoured cars, and which he was examining. The bullet lodged within a few feet of an old woman's head, she being—at least at first—an interested spectator of the scene.

Well, the orders for a march on Ostend were issued, and as nothing could be done until daybreak I went back to my room and snatched another two hours' rest. At daylight the orders went out, and in due course the first troops moved off. Then there came an order cancelling the move, and before the messengers who took the new order could be stopped there came another saying to carry on. Thus, several miles were added to the fifteen or so that the men had to do.

The general and I remained a long time after the others had gone, and then at about 11 a.m. we mounted our horses and rode on. Poor Tom, my Irish groom, was in despair because one of the others had stolen a stirrup and leather off one of my saddles during the night. Nothing is more annoying than this kind of petty pilfering, which unfortunately is only too common in the army. I sent Tom back to the stable, in which he had spent the night near the "Lion de Flandre," but all to no purpose. Tom's horse—I think it was "Sportsman"—had to be the one with only one stirrup. But Tom didn't care. He tied a loop in a piece of rope and fixed it in place of a leather, and rode quite jauntily all that journey. And at one place the general, to get past some troops at a narrow bit of roadway, leaped a ditch and we followed, all the horses jumping like stags.

It was sad riding out of Bruges, and we felt mean and as though we had been there on false pretences. The inhabitants' hospitality had been prodigious, poor people! As we rode out the crowds looked at us in a queer, silent way. There was not a cheer, for we were going west instead of east.

So scrupulous were we not to do anything in Bruges that could be fastened upon by the Germans as a pretext for increased severity towards the inhabitants that we insisted that the proprietor of the Hotel de Flandre should haul down the Red Cross flag which flew over the entrance, while we made his hotel our headquarters. This he seemed most reluctant to do. We didn't like him. He was a German, and looked as though he hated us; and he kept glass cases in his hall full of the most nauseating water-lizards, which he fed on raw meat and which ate each other when they could get nothing else to eat.

We had been warned by the Belgian authorities on our arrival that the walls had ears—especially at our hotel—and so we were extra careful. The spy peril was to be brought home to us again and again during our travels in Flanders.

But from the generality of the people we received nothing but kindness, and it was pleasant to see our men, after a long day's march, taking the wee children of their billets in their arms, and in the early morning, before they left, sweeping the floor of shop or dwelling-house and the doorstep. In Bruges I found an artillery officer's servant trying to explain to a little knot of sympathetic burgesses in the street that his master's charger was suffering from saddle galls, and that he had sent him into the town to get a sheepskin. I was able to come to the rescue and take him to a butcher. This worthy had not got a sheepskin, but he knew of an excellent man who would certainly have one. Unfortunately, he lived at some distance away, but a competent guide would be procured. I could not accompany my soldier friend and his guide (who was immediately forthcoming in the person of the first man to pass the shop). But they set off in the utmost good fellowship together, neither understanding one word that the other said.

We left Bruges by the north-west, clattering over the cobble stones, and when clear of the town we set off at a good round pace. We went by way of Scheepsdaete, Vuilvlaage, Vyfwegh, etc., and very soon caught up with the troops. We kept coming upon strings of dejected Belgian infantry, too, especially as we neared Ostend, who had been set down at various wayside stations along the railway, having just made their escape from stricken Antwerp.

The country along the route was flat and fertile, with a good deal of water.

We had arranged for our troops to take up a line of outposts some distance to the east of Ostend, and we ourselves pushed on to pick up our quarters in the town. We could see it ahead of us for a long time before we reached it, and as we drew near, we began to realise how full it was of people. The spires of a magnificent church rose grandly above the other buildings.

As we rode in along a broad street that led us over a canal with wide lock-gates, we began to meet motors full of busy British officers dashing from place to place. Crowds of refugees were everywhere, and these became denser as we approached the Gare Maritime. British cavalry were in possession of the great square in front of this station, and as we picked our way among them I noticed with an odd sense of companionship renewed that they were the 10th Hussars, whom I had known in former happy days at Rawal Pindi.

On reaching the Gare Maritime we dismounted and left our horses with the grooms in a corner of the thronged square. What Tom could have thought of the scene I cannot say. But what an experience for a young Irish country lad! My general went into the station offices, where a Council of War was being held. Sir H. Rawlinson was there and other generals, among whom I recognised General Kavanagh, whom I had known at Rawal Pindi. I remembered a grey racing pony of his called "Moneyspinner" and how on one occasion after winning a race on it he had forgotten to weigh in and we had all lost our bets. N—— (of the 13th Hussars)—poor fellow, he was shortly afterwards killed—was in a motor outside the entrance, and I got in and sat beside him to have a talk. I managed to get some lunch in the station buffet, where the "scrum" was terrific, officers and men all mixed up and about one waiter for the lot.

After many hours my general came out, and we proceeded together to our hotel the Villa Britannica. He told me that he had been given a job of work for the morrow—"a little bit of rear-guards," he said, "and we shall have some scrapping." I gradually learned from him something of what we were to do. We were to take two of our three brigades by rail to Ghent, to gain time for the garrison of Antwerp to leave, passing westwards through us.

The rest of the evening, until far on into the night, I was motoring backwards and forwards between the hotel and station. I went with D—— to an interview with the Belgian Railway Transport Staff and with the great railway expert, Sir Percy Girouard, and the whole move was arranged. The only cavalry we were to take with us was our divisional cavalry.

I did not get any dinner that night until after 11 o'clock, although I was able to arrange for some for the staff in a pretentious restaurant on the front. But at that hour I was at last free, and so, marching into the restaurant, I ordered food and drink. The lounge was full of a curious cosmopolitan crowd that looked like a shabby imitation of the *rasta-quouère* assemblage of ordinary times, but the dining-room was empty, with the lights turned off and the chairs piled one on top of the other. After manager, sub-manager, head waiter, and every other functionary had assured me that it was quite impossible to have a meal at that hour, I sat down at a table and told them that it was of supreme importance to their town that I should be fed. They thereupon produced some excellent cold chicken and tongue, also some whisky, and I ate and drank ravenously, for I was very hungry.

We were all astir very early next morning, 9th October, so early, in fact, that my servant was not there to call me or to pack my kit. Luckily, I can always call myself, however, and it was not until I was actually starting for the station that my man turned up. I told him that that day was to see us in action for the first time, and that in consequence of his lapse he would have to stop behind with the 21st Brigade, the one that was not going with us.

At the station there was a long delay. Ours was timed to be the first train to leave, and we were over an hour late in starting. The other trains were later still, and so great was the confusion that there were not wanting rumours that the upsetting of all plans and calculations was due to treachery that bugbear of all our operations in Belgium. In spite, however, of the delay, we were unable to get anything in the shape of breakfast save a cup of coffee and a piece of bread, but Vincent, one of the cooks—an excellent fellow—prepared sandwiches for us in the train.

On the way to Ghent we passed again through Bruges, and the station was crowded with people cheering frantically and pressing food and cigarettes upon the men. A party of Belgian Boy Scouts was of great service in procuring various small things for the officers.

Arrived at Ghent, we were met at the station by several officers of the Belgian General Staff, one of whom, a fine big man whose headdress was a magnificent shaggy busby, drove me to the Hotel de Ville in the wake of my general and his escort. From the Hotel de Ville steps he took me in great haste out to the *Place d'Exercice*, where our 20th Brigade was to assemble, to find Brigadier General R—— B—— and bring him back to confer with my general. As we alternately sped and crawled along the streets in our car we passed through many bodies of troops, both our own and French, the latter being parties of marines—fine, wild-looking Bretons. But it was sad to meet, coming in the opposite direction, long strings of refugees from Antwerp and the burning villages nearer to Ghent.

"Refugees, tears, enthusiasm, pluck, pathos" is the entry in my little notebook.

Thanks to his staff cap, I readily saw General R—— B——, and getting him into the car, we returned to the Town Hall.

That was a very wonderful first day in Ghent.

"My first battle?" is the entry I see in my notebook (I cannot call it a diary, for most of the entries are of this kind: "Paid 10 *francs* 50 *cents.* for breakfast of staff"). But there was no fighting that day. Our men got into position, covering Ghent from attack from the east, southeast and south, from about the Lokeren-Loochristy-Ghent road to the Melle-Ghent road. The French marines were on their right, and the Belgians, moving back from Antwerp to Eecloo, on their left. The 22nd Brigade had its headquarters in an inn at the junction of the roads from Deynze and Eecke, while the 20th had its headquarters near the first kilometre stone on the Ghent-Destelbergen Road. Our headquarters were, as I have said, at the Hotel de Ville, and there the willing authorities fixed us up a complete telephonic installation by which we were in direct communication with our two brigades, with Ostend, and even (I think) with the War Office. The Belgian *quartier-général* was nearby.

The Hotel de Ville is a very beautiful building, and we had our headquarters in its Council Chamber. It is of grey stone, in the Gothic style, and is one of a striking cluster which encloses, as it were, the soul of the city. Quite close to it is the soaring belfry, in whose high summit there is a marvellous peal of bells. A little farther away is the church of St. Bavon, patron saint of Ghent. Over the belfry, with its dizzy "extinguisher" tops and mediaeval air, the flag of Belgium floated proudly.

The Grand Council Chamber was a room of massive proportions, with high windows all down one side looking out upon a quiet quadrangle, and opposite the windows was a huge fireplace, with what I imagined to be a valuable Old Flemish Master above it. A baize-covered table ran down the centre of the room almost its whole length, and the walls were panelled in oak, the ceiling, if I recollect aright, being of oak too. One entered from double doors down a few steps and there was a small room leading from the big one, into which my general later on retired when the bustle and telephoning had got on his nerves. All through that day and the next workmen were busy in the quadrangle, taking volumes from the library opposite and carrying them down to some mysterious cellar. It was a pitiable thing to watch. The *burgomaster* and town authorities were probably aware that we could not long hold Ghent, and they knew what had come to Louvain!

Outside the Council Chamber there were many smaller rooms, and perhaps rooms as big, or bigger for all we knew. I noticed that the civil work was going on just the same as usual the day we arrived. There were suitors and witnesses—all the crowd incidental to the administration of Justice. But on the second day there was nothing save the military and a few furtive charwomen.

Many Belgian officers, bearers of dispatches, came to our headquarters throughout that day (9th October). One of these Belgian dispatches was from Ostend, and it laid down the policy to be pursued by our division. We were to cover the withdrawal from Antwerp of the Belgian Army and of our Naval Brigade. If the latter could be moved by rail, they would be sent that morning to Ostend and there be clear of our sphere of operations. The Belgian Field Army, for the protection of which we were made responsible, would endeavour to effect its withdrawal to some point on the line Lille-Dunkirk, to enable it to recuperate in France.

The task of protecting the Belgian Field Army was to be fulfilled thus: we were to protect their rear, as they retired, while the French, by holding successively the passages of the Lys, were to protect their eastern flank as they (the Belgians) marched south-westward.

Interruption to the march of the Belgians was most to be looked for from enemy forces which were known to be in the neighbourhood of Tournai, Courtrai and Audenarde. Should this assumption prove correct, the Belgian Army would have to change its line of march to the westward, nearer the sea.

At mid-day we were made acquainted in detail with the actual position of the Belgian Army. Four divisions of infantry had retired to the western bank of the Ghent-Terneuzen Canal, between Salzaete and Mariakerke, and were there reorganising. A few detachments, of both cavalry and infantry, supported by artillery, were on the eastern bank of the canal, while the entire Belgian Cavalry Division had been ordered to proceed towards Lokeren, to delay the enemy who had been reported there on the previous evening (8th).

It was definitely stated that our Naval Brigade had left Antwerp on the evening of the 8th "in order to join the Field Army," and that the first trainloads of them had left St. Gilles Waes this morning for Ostend and Zeebrugge. It was also stated, though less definitely, that the 2nd Belgian Division had likewise made good its escape from Antwerp.

Finally, it was urged by the Belgians that, since the protection of Ghent from the south appeared to be sufficient for the moment, our troops (including the cavalry at Eecloo) should be pushed up the Ghent-Lokeren road to cooperate with the Belgian Cavalry Division in protecting the withdrawal of our Naval Brigade and the Belgian 2nd Division. This seemed to the Belgian General Staff the most urgent task for the moment. It was, however, stated that should the situation south of Ghent become more threatening later on this plan would have to be altered.

Later in the day we received news of cavalry and motor machine-gun engagements between Loochristy and Overmeire, the latter place being considerably this side of Lokeren, and of the falling back of the Belgian cavalry from St. Amand to the north-east of Ghent. Then we heard that the enemy had been seen on the left bank of the Scheldt, in the woods near Melle, and the French marines in that portion of the line were reported to be running short of ammunition.

In fact, it soon appeared that the enemy was threatening Ghent from the south as well as from the east. We remained in our positions.

D——, who was all day at the Gare St. Pierre, telephoned in the afternoon to say that the transport of units was only arriving very slowly, and that no artillery had yet arrived from Ostend.

Late that night we received copies of the orders issued by the Belgian General Headquarters at Eecloo for the continuation of their withdrawal on the morrow, 10th October. This withdrawal was to be to the district about Thourout, Ghistelles, Ostend, etc., and General Headquarters were to be at the latter place by 8 a.m. on the 10th.

I was much struck by the quiet, resolute mien of all the Belgian officers who brought reports and dispatches. Especially do I remember a young cavalry captain who looked as though he had just taken part in a peaceful jumping competition at Olympia. The Belgians and French always wore their peace uniform at that time, though the French officers, I noticed later on at Ypres, had discarded all their gold lace and were dressed exactly like their men.

There is always something fascinating to one who has not yet been under fire, but who knows that he soon will be, in hearing the impressions of anybody who quite lately has been under it. This young cavalry officer had only left Antwerp that morning, and had been in all the fighting, including that at Liege. All the Belgian officers seemed mightily pleased at our arrival, but I think they were grievously disappointed when they realised the smallness of our force.

Here I must anticipate a bit, and declare that though the Belgian retirement from Antwerp to behind the shelter afforded by our little force was precipitate, and necessarily so, yet when we ourselves had to leg it westwards large forces of Belgian cavalry covered both their own infantry's retreat and ours. Indeed, there was a time, just as we left Thielt, on the 13th October, when but for a good fight put up by the Belgian cavalry we must have been badly harassed by the pursuing Germans.

CHAPTER 4

Ghent and Afterwards

To return to the 9th October. The day wore on without our troops being engaged, though various *Uhlan* patrols were sighted. In the afternoon I had to go to the Hotel de la Poste, in the Place d'Armes, to arrange billets for all the Headquarters group. As it turned out we never used them, though we took some of our meals there. There were some wounded Belgian officers and men being looked after on the top floor, and some of the convalescents and the nurses dined in the hotel dining-room. There was one absolute Venus of a nurse. We all considered the Continental Red Cross uniform far more becoming than our own.

I dined at the hotel on all three nights of our stay in Ghent, and it was either on the first or second night that I noticed a small party of English-speaking men seated at a table near mine. They were of a kind known in South Africa as "scallywags," and one at least was a peculiarly disagreeable specimen of the breed. He seems to be found wherever war has caused the overthrow of law and order, never really risking his life, but battening on the deaths and miseries of others. There was a young man with him who, seeing that I was a British officer, came up and spoke to me. I gathered that he was doing work for one of the big cinema agencies, and that he had secured some marvellous films.

He was an American, I think, or possessed an American passport. I remember he told me that he had several times been searched by the Germans, and he gave me what he meant to be a very useful hint. "The Germans," he said, "never search your cap. Boots, yes; clothes, yes; *but not your cap.*" He was not so bad, but unfortunately his sinister-looking companion came up, more than a little drunk, and insisted on shaking hands with me too. There was something most unpleasant about him, and the worst of it was that he hinted that he had some sort of connection with the Red Cross. What exactly he meant when he said to me "I have killed many of them" (meaning German officers) I don't know, and didn't care to guess. He nodded with a mixture of grimness and slyness. Again, he repeated "Many of them," and he pulled up his sleeve and showed me a pair of heavy gold engraved sleeve-links, and then drew a dirty forefinger across his throat.

Colonel S——, of the R.A.M.C., and I had a real piece of luck that night, just as it appeared that we should have to spend the night on mattresses on the floor of the Council Chamber. Young de Kherkhove (son of the Governor of Ghent), who had offered his services to us as interpreter and guide, told us he could get us put up in the house of a friend, a M. Feyrick, in the Rue Neuve St. Pierre. Thither we made our way, for *"Be as comfortable as you can be"* is the motto of a good campaigner, and we found our host only too delighted to do anything he could for us. He gave us a bedroom each, with the most comfortable of beds, and though we were only allowed a bare three hours' sleep that night it was like sleeping in Paradise. The entry in my notebook runs:

After three hours' sleep in real luxury, up at 3.30. Harassing morning. Day petered out.

All the same we heard that day that the French marines had repulsed an attack by Germans to the south of Ghent and killed six hundred of them.

But at that early hour of the morning it seemed certain we were in for a big battle, and our horses were outside the Hotel de Ville, saddled and waiting in the cold darkness. Yet nothing much happened, and I took the opportunity of beginning a letter home.

I think it was that morning, at about 9 o'clock, that a couple of British Army aviators arrived from Ostend to report to my general. One of them came up and spoke to me. He was a gunner, whom I had not seen since the summer of 1910, at Kailana, in the Indian hills. We had played polo there together, and I remembered that I had much admired a chestnut Arab pony of his and had thought of buying it from him when he went home. I asked him about it now.

What a thing to hark back to at such a time and on this chance isolated meeting! But such is the way in the army. I asked him if he had had breakfast.

"Oh, no," he said, "we are going back to Ostend for breakfast."

What had taken us some hours by train would take them only a few minutes by air.

After this meeting I went out to see the Cathedral of St. Bavon. It was a magnificent sight, but as my eye travelled up those lofty columns, and lost itself in the gothic obscurity of the roof, I saw in imagination great holes and rents and crumblings all round—the brutal work of the Beast.

I wanted to have someone else appreciate it too, and I thought of Tom Condon, my Irish groom who, after standing for long hours with the horses waiting for us to mount, had been ordered back to the *Cercle*, in which was situated the great riding-school wherein they were stabled. So, I went in one of the motors and fetched him.

I took him with me in the car, not telling him where we were going, and when we arrived at the steps of the Hotel de Ville we got out and I said "Tom, do you want to see the finest church you ever saw in your life?"

"I do," he said.

So, I led the way across the square and into the great church. The day was beginning to fade, but there was still enough light to see by, and together we walked round, and knelt for a moment in prayer.

My colonel friend and I found the same good quarters that night as the night before, but this time we had six hours' sleep instead of three, and badly we needed them. At 6 in the morning of Sunday, 11th October, we woke to the sound of heavy musketry to the east. But the mist came on very thickly, and presently the firing ceased. We had luxurious hot baths, and our kind host again gave us breakfast, and insisted not only on being present at the meal, but on driving us in his motor to the Hotel de Ville.

As the morning wore on news came that the enemy was advancing in force towards us. We heard that a division of Belgian cavalry was retiring slowly before him, and that great part of the British Naval Brigade had lost its way and wandered into Holland. The *burgomaster* waited upon my general to beg that if we were going to retire, we might do so before the Germans shelled his city. My general replied that he would hate to see the city shelled, but that he must carry out his instructions. Needless to say, we had to keep all our projected movements secret, as far as possible, for spies swarmed everywhere.

During the morning a party of Gordon Highlanders marched in three German prisoners that they had taken. The three (the first I had seen) sat on a bench outside the Council Chamber, and looked stolidly indifferent to their surroundings, until quite suddenly one of them started to blubber. They were Saxons—great, stupid, stolid peasants. I had witnessed their arrival at the Hotel de Ville a little while before. A dreadful cry, as of a wild beast, had gone up from the crowd that thronged the square—a cry of rage and pain, of despair and hatred; for that crowd was swelled by many homeless refugees who were at that moment flocking in from the ravaged country to the east. It was a feminine cry, if there was sex in it at all. I did not wonder that the Saxon booby cried.

I was able to get away for an hour during that Sunday morning to hear Mass in the cathedral. Never shall I forget the scene. The day was dark, and an immense dark congregation was assembled. The only spot of light and colour was the beautiful altar of St. Bavon, in front of which were burning innumerable wax candles, and which was draped with a huge Belgian flag. It is a combination of colours, that black, yellow, red, that seems to glow and about which there can be nothing cold. That flag glowed and flamed, over there across the spaces of the transept. Suddenly there was a dull boom, and from that moment to the end of Mass one heard the distant cannon thundering.

At each report a shiver went through the congregation, and when a priest ascended the pulpit to preach one felt and knew that the air was charged with emotion. All between the pulpit and the high altar turned their chairs to face the preacher, and I felt my heart full of sorrow for those poor women and old men, as I saw the faces they raised to listen to the sermon.

The preacher spoke in Flemish, so that I understood scarcely a word. But it was not hard to imagine what he was saying. At one point, during a pause, the sound of cannon came menacingly loud. He faltered on the beginning of a fresh sentence, and many people sobbed without restraint.

When the sermon was over, the usual poor old woman of the Belgian churches came round with the collecting box. I tried to put a piece of money into it, but she withheld the box from me, as she also did in the case of a Belgian soldier who stood beside me.

On returning to the Council Chamber I told my general where I had been.

"I wish I could find time to see the churches," he said.

But already preparations had to be made for our evacuation of the town. After helping to write orders, I went off to the Hotel de la Poste, to sign a voucher for the quarters we had never used. Eleven that night was the hour fixed for our departure.

There was an indescribable air of romance about our three days' visit to Ghent. It was an anxious time, however, and one of great fatigue for our men, practically all of whom were on continuous outpost duty, day and night. One poor officer, Egerton, of the Border Regiment, had to be left behind, and died soon afterwards. We heard that he had been out in front of his outposts during the night, and got shot through the lungs. Poor fellow, he was in my Militia years ago, and we had been great friends.

On the first night there had nearly been an ugly incident, and but for the coolness of the men of our 22nd Brigade there would have been one. Some neighbouring troops blazed off most of their ammunition at our trenches, but luckily our men lay low, and only lost two of their number wounded.

Spies were everywhere, and our outposts were dreadfully bothered by them. Left to themselves, how were they to distinguish between an ordinary refugee and a spy? The civil police helped them to a great extent. But even when a supposed spy was caught, and his guilt to all intents and purposes established, what could we do to punish him? We were not ruthless like the Germans, and the benefit of the doubt was freely given. Yet some were forced to accompany us in our retirement that would far better have been shot out of hand, their guilt being clear. During our subsequent forced marches, I used to see one especially, as I rode along the column, to whom our pitying men had lent a great-coat to keep him warm.

On the afternoon of the day of our departure from Ghent, as I was leaving the Council Chamber on some business or other, I ran into a poor lady who, with her husband, had come to intercede for her son. He had just been brought in from our outposts, where he had been caught red-handed signalling to the enemy. The woman was in tears, and kept insisting that her son was incapable of such a thing, and that he was feeble-minded. I could only assure her that he would have a fair trial. Unfortunately, it was often the feebleminded that the Germans made use of for their dirty work. I never heard what happened to the boy.

It was always part of my duty to see that no documents or messages were left behind that might be of service to the enemy, and so I was the last of the staff to leave the Town Hall. I burned in the great fireplace many discarded memoranda, etc., and as I left, I heard for the last time the sweet chimes of the belfry ringing through the oak-panelled rooms and corridors. It seemed as though one could detect a note of uneasiness and foreboding in them. Heaven grant that the *Kaiser's* legions may spare the architectural beauties of Ghent and Bruges! It has always seemed to me that the voice of educated opinion in the United States might with advantage be raised in this matter. Surely their comfortable fetish of neutrality would not be violated by such a remonstrance! (The date on which this was written must be borne in mind—Author.)

It was 11 o'clock that night when we moved silently off from the Hotel de Ville towards the starting point. We were on foot, our horses being led in rear of us. There was a very long delay in the bitter cold when we got there, and for a time the French marines were badly mixed up with our columns. A French horse slipped and fell on the cobble-stones, and blocked the march of our column until one of our officers ran forward and laid a blanket in front of him which enabled him to get sufficient purchase to rise to his feet again. However, in the end the long trudge westward was in full swing. It was to go on all that night and nearly all the next day.

That night march was a most miserable affair, and what made it worse was that the men were tired out even before they started. For they had had nothing approaching real rest since they landed. At Bruges they were continuously on outpost duty. At Ostend their only night was spent in great discomfort. At Ghent they had lived in a state of continuous tension and alarm.

We had scarcely gone five miles when individual men began to drop out. Whenever a halt was ordered the men lay down at once on the side of the road—a certain indication of fatigue. All were possessed by an almost uncontrollable desire to sleep. I had experienced a combination of intense cold and utter weariness on a night march once before in my life, between Peshawar and Rawal Pindi; but it was not as bad as this. After a time, I simply could not keep awake, and found myself at every few paces swaying right across the road.

At last I tried getting up on one of my horses for a bit, and then walking again; and to my great satisfaction I found that I had lost the intense craving for sleep. But when we had gone about eight miles the men started falling out in parties of threes and fours. I could see them just quietly leaving the ranks and sitting down on the side of a steep bank that ran down from the roadway; and no efforts of entreaty or upbraiding on the part of their officers could move them. Poor officers! They were just as tired themselves. The 22nd Brigade was the one we were with—where the 20th was marching I cannot recall;

they were ahead of us, I think, or marching on a parallel road farther north.

Just as it was beginning to get light, we heard that portion of our force had taken a wrong turning. I had to jump into a motorcar and go in pursuit. I took Kherkhove and a young gunner officer with me and we followed the strayed party by the tracks of their guns. Eventually it appeared that they had taken a turning which would lead them back to the main road again. We followed, and came up with them just as they had joined on. It was now daylight—a misty, cold morning—and we had reached a little village called Hansbeke, where we halted.

The good people of the village (it had only 3,000 inhabitants) vied with one another in serving coffee to officers and men, nor would they hear of payment. I got coffee, *tartines* and eggs in a neat little house, where the kind hostess could not do enough for me when she heard that I was Irish and a Catholic. I told her my groom was the same, and at once she begged me to send him in. So, thanking her, I went out into the yard to hold the horses, and sent Tom in to breakfast. She, too, would not hear of payment; but I persuaded her at last to accept a little present to put by for the baby that was in the cradle.

My general and the rest of the staff had ridden on to a big *château* outside the village of Bellem, and thither I followed them. It was the residence of Kherkhove's father, Governor of Ghent, and a place of some magnificence. I was just in time to induce my general to eat a bit of breakfast (always a difficult task with him) before he settled down to the writing of fresh orders with his two senior general staff officers. D—— and I, having seen to our horses, went to look for a spot in the garden where we could lay our waterproof sheets and greatcoats on the grass and doze. The sun was now shining brightly, but the grass was still drenched with dew. We selected a sunny corner of the lawn and had just settled down to sleep when I heard my name called loudly.

Chapter 5

Going West

I had a "job of work" to do. Alarming reports had just come in that the enemy was driving back the screen of Belgian cavalry that was operating between us and Ghent, and some of our own 3rd Cavalry Division, under General Byng, was in touch with him away on our right, *i.e.* to the south. We could hear our Horse Artillery guns engaging him at that moment.

The general gave me rapid orders, and told me that there was no time to be lost. The 22nd Brigade was to reinforce its detachments that were already holding certain points in our rear along the Lys Canal. I was to visit these points, reconnoitre the whole of our defensive line from Nevele to about Lovendegem, and report. I was to visit Brigadier-General L——'s headquarters in Hansbeke on my way, give him certain orders, and request his presence at Divisional Headquarters immediately.

General L——'s motor was standing near the spot at which I met him, and we got into it to look at the map in greater comfort. He was distressed at having to call upon his men for further efforts, as they were quite done. Yet the orders I conveyed to him might have entailed the sacrifice of all his outposts had the Belgian cavalry screen been driven in and the enemy acted more vigorously. He was to hold on to Nevele at all costs, to Hansbeke (where we now were), and to all the canal crossings between Nevele and Lovendegem. I was to tell him that:

It was most important we should get to Thielt this (12th October) evening. G.O.C. cannot afford to turn to fight, therefore L—— must hold on. Nevele is his right flank, Lovendegem is his left. Transport to be loaded up and sent to Thielt, with a few cyclists as escort. He must arrange some means of communication with Divisional Headquarters. All his posts *must* hold on.

General L—— assured me his posts could not hope to resist an attack in any force. I said, would he go to Headquarters and tell the general so? I mounted my horse ("Dawn") again and galloped off to Nevele, and he went by motor to Headquarters.

As I went, I could hear the guns firing in the direction of Courtrai, but there was no sound of firing to our front. On my way I met several squadrons of Belgian cavalry retiring, and they told me they were only doing so after being relieved by others. They were mostly on the wrong side of the road (the left), but quite cheerful, and their horses in fair condition. They made a brave show in their blue and red uniforms. To cut a big corner at one point I put the mare at a ditch, which she jumped beautifully. They cheered me. "*Officier d'Etat-Major anglais,*" I heard them say.

I found the little village of Nevele crowded with Belgian cavalry and civilians, and I made my way across the canal bridge to find the officer in command of the British Force. This was D——, of the South Staffords. He had with him five subalterns, two hundred rank and file, and two machine-guns. I made due note of his dispositions. He struck me as being the right man for the job. He brought me to the Headquarters of the Belgian Cavalry *commandant*.

It was 11.35 a.m. when I reached D——, and I could not get away from the Belgian Headquarters till 12.35. I had some difficulty in finding the *commandant*, but when I did, he most courteously lent me a copy of his orders, which I took down. The Lys was being guarded by a Belgian cavalry division at its bridges and fords, between the two railways, Ghent-Bruges and Deynze-Thielt. Two companies of cyclists and one squadron 5th Lancers were guarding the immediate neighbourhood of the "*pont rayé*" of Tronchiennes, and the bridge at Laethem St. Martin. A *peloton* of cyclists and a *peloton* of cavalry with a machine-gun were assigned to each of these bridges, the remainder being in reserve at Baerle. The third company of cyclists and one squadron of the 4th Lancers at Poucques (the headquarters of the Cavalry Division) guarded the bridge over the Lys at Deynze, near the clock-tower, and the railway bridge at Grammene. Reserve towards Zeveren.

The 3rd Battery of artillery was watching the approaches to the south-east of Deynze and the debouches from Deynze to the north-west. In the same manner batteries stationed at Poesele were watching

Men of the 7th reading newspapers from home, during a wayside halt, near Ypres, October, 1914

to the south-east of Nevele, towards Deurle.

Should the cavalry patrols be driven in they were to be reinforced by three squadrons at Nevele (where we then were), and three at Lootenhulle.

I thanked the Belgian *commandant*, and mounted my mare at 12.35, choosing the western bank of the canal. I got to Landegem Bridge at 12.45, and met B—— and eighteen troopers of the Northumberland Hussars, our divisional cavalry. While crossing the railway above Landegem I saw the British Naval Brigade armoured train standing on the line. I rode along the embankment to interview the commander, Robinson. A more business-like lot of men than the Jack Tars that manned it it would be impossible to imagine. I had instructions for Robinson, and while I was giving him these, I had to get a tar to hold my horse. He did this rather gingerly, remarking that he was not used to such "a ticklish job!" A train-load of refugees came from the Ghent direction, and I hastened to resume possession of my horse and lead him down the embankment.

Proceeding along the canal, I found a squadron of the Northumberland Hussars at Meerendre Bridge, under Major C——. He told me he was to report to the O.C. Welsh Fusiliers at 1.15. As I rode on an aeroplane passed over at a great height, going west. I think it was a French Maurice Farman. At 1.40 I arrived at Lovendegem, which is about two miles east of the Lys Canal, and on the much bigger Canal de Gand. I found it held by three of our men. One was a lance-corporal, and he told me that only thirty Germans had been reported in Ghent that morning. I noted that the bridge and complicated set of locks where the larger canal crossed the smaller were commanded by an embankment on the east bank of the latter. A kindly person gave me a foaming glass of beer, and I cantered on under the splendid trees along the northern bank of the large canal, to regain our Headquarters at Bellem.

As I moved along the soft track, I saw a party of peasants approaching from the opposite direction. There were about half-a-dozen of them, men and women, and as soon as they espied me, I saw them take cover behind the trees. As I got nearer, they started peering out at me in a most ludicrous manner. They probably took me for a German. I reassured them and they seemed very much relieved. It was 2 o'clock when I came to Hanime Bridge, and turned away from the canal towards Bellem. At the bridge I came upon Captain J—— and a subaltern and one hundred and forty men, of the Welsh Fusiliers, I think, guarding the approach from the north.

Shortly afterwards I got back to the Kherkhove Château, only to find that Headquarters had moved on. Much disgusted, for I was full of my mission, and also very tired (horse and man), I rode on to the village of Bellem, where I found my general established with his staff in the post-office. He was telephoning through to some place north of Bruges, where it appeared that the 21st Brigade, which we had left behind at Ostend, now were. He was ordering them to effect a junction with us at Thielt. I made my report, much of which had by now become unnecessary. It seemed evident to me that General L——'s remonstrance had had its effect, and that the G.O.C. had decided not to attempt any rear-guard fighting, but to push on to Thielt under cover of the Belgian cavalry screen, and of our own.

We therefore continued our march, at about 4 p.m., and with utterly exhausted men. We marched through Aeltre and Ruysselede, and arrived at Thielt at about 7. It was a fatiguing march, with little of interest about it. If anything, the little shrines at the cross-roads and street corners were more numerous than they had been nearer Ghent. I remember, too, the name over one inn: "*In de Springende Peerd*," "At the Sign of the Prancing Horse," and the words reminded me forcibly of Cape Dutch. It occurred to me, too, that we might, with a little *bandobast*, have utilised the steam tramway which ran alongside the road for the conveyance of our weary infantry. I had seen several trains full of civilians passing, and it would not have been very difficult to arrange. I mentioned the idea to my general the next day, but the suggestion was too late to be of any use. I feel pretty sure, though, that the Germans who were following us utilised this ready-to-hand means of locomotion, for they were in Thielt next day almost before we had left it, and hard on our heels.

I shall never forget the last half mile or so of our march into Thielt. The poor, tired infantry were brought to a halt for half hours at a time. Some of them were from two to three hours in completing that last half mile. To those who know what such halts mean to weary men at the end of a march and in sight of their billets—halting for an indefinite time, then moving on a few paces, halting again, and never allowed to fall out and relax—I need not say that our infantry were utterly "fed up." Luckily the weather kept fine, and the additional discomfort of rain was not added to their troubles.

I had never wholly succeeded in catching the general up since we left Bellem. It was very dark for the last portion of the march, and unless one has a particular reason one should refrain from riding past troops on the march. But when we encountered the check above described in the streets of Thielt I felt it necessary to push on. I arrived at the Town Hall at about 7 o'clock, and then went on a little farther to seek a stable for my horse.

Horses were being billeted all down one street, in large courtyards. The confusion was very great, and at first, I had to have my three separated, but later on my groom and servant between them contrived to have them all together.

After securing supper for my general and all the staff in the only restaurant in the place, I got a *billet de logement* through one of our Belgian interpreters, for I had no mind to pass the night on the floor of the Hotel de Ville. Had I known at what a distance the house was I doubt whether I would have thought it worthwhile, for I was very tired and we had to be off betimes in the morning. The name of my host-to-be was, as far as I could catch it, Monsiri Edile, and I suppose it must have been the latter name that made me think he was some sort of official connected with the town.

I procured a guide in the person of about the queerest little man I have ever set eyes on. He was very small and pale and dressed all in black. He had side-whiskers and wore a large bowler hat. He assured me it was very little distance to the Edile dwelling, and we set out along a street that was crowded with our soldiers.

There was a curious sense in Thielt of being in an Italian hill town. It certainly is raised considerably above the surrounding country, being marked on the Ordnance map 40 metres, whereas Pitthem and other little towns in the vicinity are only about 25. It was a long kilometre to my destination, as it turned out, and as I was carrying my greatcoat it seemed every bit of that. I walked along with the little man, while my servant, who disapproved of the whole business, brought up the rear.

Never have I met anybody so timid as my little guide. Whenever we had to pass near the hindquarters of a horse he would make as wide a detour as possible to avoid them, and a man handling a bayonet made his knees quake under him. As these things occurred at every few yards our progress was naturally slow.

As we proceeded, I began to doubt whether he was really conducting me to Monsiri Edile's at all. I became very angry with his timidity, and at times to get him on I had to threaten him with violence. He could not speak more than about three words of French, and the only

English he knew was "station," which word, however, he didn't mention until we had got some distance. It suddenly occurred to me that he might have thought that I wanted to go to the station, and I tried to explain to him that I did not. But he only kept repeating the word "station," and so with many misgivings, but hoping for the best, I kept on. Luckily it was downhill, and at last, just as we came in sight of the station lights, my guide crossed over the road to a little public-house, and said "Monsiri Edile." We had arrived! I thanked the poor little man and we entered.

The proprietor was most obliging, and said that if I would sit down for a while, he would get my room ready for me. The little guide withdrew, and left me and my servant in the company of a couple of loafers in the tap-room. Then I was shown up a rickety staircase to my room. I think it must have belonged to the proprietor himself. It was reasonably clean and the bed was very comfortable, and what more could a tired man wish for in the circumstances? My servant's disapproval, however, by no means vanished when the good lady of the house came in to see the unusual visitor—a British staff officer—accompanied by her three daughters in their nightgowns!

They told me in voluble but very bad French that there were two French officers billeted in the next room to me, and each of them carried off a different article of my equipment (except my revolver) to clean. I hope my servant was reassured by the wax sacred images that stood in glass cases on the mantelpiece. Anyhow, he withdrew somewhat doubtfully to return to the Town Hall. I told him the proprietor would awaken me early, and that he was to be ready for me in the morning at the Town Hall, with Tom and the horses.

I slept like a log that night, but was up even before the proprietor came to awaken me. Breakfast of coffee and *tartines* was prepared for me downstairs, and a very moderate sum charged for bed and board. I set out, much refreshed, for the Town Hall, and got breakfast ready in the little restaurant for my general and the remainder of the staff. We were soon on the road again, all three brigades (for we had been joined the evening before by the 21st Brigade), and setting out for Roulers. This was the morning of the 13th October.

That the Germans did not shell us while we were in Thielt I think must in great measure be ascribed to the fine covering work done by the Belgian cavalry. Had they done so the slaughter would have been terrible. Thielt, though a tiny town, contains about 11,500 inhabitants, and we had a very large number of men crammed and packed into it. Even a Taube dropping bombs must have worked havoc. What a chance they missed!

Our first halt was at Pitthem, and there we had a very long delay. It came on to rain heavily, and the men were wet through and miserably cold. Headquarters waited for about two hours in an inn which possessed a tiny billiard-table over which was written in Flemish what we took to be "Fluke not: God sees you!" (*Vlook*, I believe, really means "swear"!)

I was sent careering on by the general to recall the advanced guard, which was taking the road to Ardoye, and to give orders that only the baggage was to go that way, while the column struck off farther to the south. Shortly afterwards a Belgian officer arrived with the news that the Germans were in Thielt, and that one of our heavy motor-lorries was lying abandoned in the ditch just this side of the town. The general told me to go back to see what could be done about it. He said I was to take his motorcar but to be very careful not to get it or myself captured. I took Kherkhove with me, and three privates as escort. When we got to within about half a mile of the town, we met some retreating Belgian cavalry. They told us that they had salved the lorry by attaching it to one of theirs, and that our men before abandoning it had removed the magneto. They said they would take it with them that night to Lichtervelde—a very friendly act. They told us that their cavalry had just been heavily engaged with the Germans to the northeast of Thielt, and that they had been severely handled.

Shortly after I had returned to the general, we moved on towards Roulers. Long before we got there it was dark, and the men were dead beat. One must know what those West Flanders roads are like to understand how soon they can tire the men out in heavy weather. Only a strip, about eight feet wide, in the centre of the road, is metalled: the rest is deep in mud, or if at one side there is a tram-line, it is impossible for a horse to keep his footing there in the dark, because of the sleepers. Another thing this campaign proved to me was that when it is a matter of dealing with really exhausted men a single night's rest, or even two nights' rest (unless in the same place), is of little use. Here they had slept at Thielt, and for this night they were to sleep at Roulers; but in both cases quite a short march on the day following knocked all the stuffing out of them.

As we approached Roulers the halts became more frequent, and when they halted the men just dropped in their tracks, in the deep mud and slush, without even troubling to get to the side of the road and comparative dryness. To the catch-cry, too, of "Are we down-hearted?" (which never yet had failed to evoke a chorus of "No!"—uttered sometimes, it is true, in a very minor key) no answer at all was given. Never once, though, have I heard anybody shout "Yes!"

In the darkness the general had become detached from his staff, and search how I might, up or down the column, I could not find him. So, I pushed on into Roulers, and as the main road became completely blocked with troops I and an officer, who was dressed in a wonderful waterproof suit, of his own invention, apparently, rode through the town by devious ways, and at last arrived in front of the Town Hall. My excellent groom soon came up to look for me, with my second horse and the third one, which my servant always led with the baggage-train. He took the three to the stables that had been allotted to us, while I entered the Town Hall to find my general.

I found that our Divisional Headquarters were not there, but elsewhere. In the Town Hall the Headquarters of the 4th Corps were established, and in a very noble room upstairs, in a blaze of light, many officers of high rank were deliberating. It did not take me long to find our abode, which was down a side street leading out of the Grande Place, and a large private dwelling belonging to a most amiable old lady. I tried for a billet in the house of a rich jute merchant (jute seemed the principal industry of this fine town of 25,000 inhabitants), who hospitably gave me a whisky-and-soda, while his chief-of-staff, as it were, came in in his shirt sleeves to talk. Just as I was arranging for a night's lodging there was a loud rap on the door, and two Guards officers entered. They, too, were looking for billets, and when I heard that the whole of that street had been allotted to their regiment I, of course, withdrew.

The gentleman who had brought me to the house thereupon said he would put me up in his, some distance away, but nearer to our Headquarters than this one; and thither accordingly we departed. I found it a brand-new house, with everything in it brand-new. These Belgian town houses must cost a great deal to furnish, but somehow, they never seem to achieve real comfort. This one was no exception. It was one mass of huge modern gilt mirrors, costly new panelling, polished floors, marble stairs, etc., but it was not our idea of a home. I do not mean this by way of cavil, for nobody could have been kinder to me than my host and hostess. I think the lady told me the rooms were exact copies of some at Versailles.

I must record, however, that the owner evinced the most lively interest in all our movements. That, perhaps, was not to be wondered at, considering how much it meant to him whether we advanced on the morrow or retired. But when it came to his being up and about before I was, and out to see whether the cavalry horses that were picketed in a small square near his house were being saddled up or not, things began to look a bit suspicious—especially as I was up at four. But once again I had the luxury of a hot bath (in a marble bath this time) and a decent shave, and was able to take the road refreshed and restored.

The old lady in whose hospitable house most of the staff lodged did everybody very well. We had an excellent dinner and breakfast, and when on our departure I asked her to let me know to what extent we were indebted to her she would not accept a *sou*. She only asked for some little souvenir of our visit, and I gave her an old regimental badge which I had, with which she was delighted. I only hope the Germans did not catch the poor old body with it afterwards.

CHAPTER 6

At Bay At Ypres

Still continuing our retreat, we left Roulers early on the morning of the 14th October, but not before we had made arrangements for sending our worst cases of footsoreness, etc., to Ypres by train. It was about a 12 to 14 miles' march by the way we were going, it was raining hard, and the road was certain to be heavy.

In the circumstances it might have been better if we had decided to go round by the main road that runs at first N.W. from Roulers for about three miles, and then S.W. to Westroosebeke; but we went instead by the shortest route, *via* Oostnieuwkerke, and the saving in distance was quite outweighed by the much worse state of the road. The men had recovered much of their wonted cheerfulness on this day, and during one of the halts I heard a company singing. The air was that of "Home, Sweet Home." The words were (four lines to song):—

We're here because we're here,
We're here because we're here;
We're here because we're here,
We're here because we're here!

I see from my notebook that we did not get to Ypres until the afternoon, but I think it must have been before the hour mentioned in the following entry:—

14.10.14. 4.45 p.m. On *Place* at Ypres. Wonderful Town Hall. Coats of arms on roof. Aeroplane prisoners.

Ypres is (or, alas, was) a very beautiful and quaint old town, containing wonderful buildings. The Place d'Armes is the centre of the town, and along great portion of this is the historic building variously known as the Halles, the Linen Hall, the Markets, the Cloth Hall, and the Town Hall. This building struck my fancy in a way impossible to describe. In its vast ground-level vaulted chamber hundreds of horses were stabled, while above in the great frescoed galleries soldiers were billeted. It was of grey stone, with a lofty belfry that was in process of restoration, and to which the scaffolding still clung. The roof was of enormous extent, sloping down over the walls from a great height, and on it, gleaming in the sun, were four painted escutcheons of the ancient Counts of Flanders. Behind the Town Hall was the Cathedral of St. Martin, a noble edifice. The houses round the square were all old, and had gables and overhanging eaves, and sun-blistered shutters opening flat against their walls. I marvelled greatly that I had scarcely even heard of Ypres; it was so beautiful.

A hostile aeroplane had been brought down that morning by our Horse Artillery (of the 3rd Cavalry Division), and shortly after we entered Ypres it was brought in in triumph on a motor-lorry. I think there were two prisoners with it. They had been captured hiding in a wood.

Later in the evening I was sitting in the window of my billet, high up over the square, when I heard the clatter of many hoofs on the cobblestones below. I looked out, and saw it was a troop of the 10th Hussars, who had brought in some *Uhlan* prisoners. The fading light glinted from the drawn swords of the escort, and the whole setting of the scene was picturesque in the extreme. (Our advanced parties had found *Uhlan* patrols actually in Ypres—Author.)

We spent the whole of the 15th quietly enough in Ypres. In the Town Hall I saw the *frescoes*, depicting incidents in the history of the city, from the date of the defeat of the English long ago down to our own day. These *frescoes* were either modern, or restored for about half the length of the great hall, and for the other half they were old and faded. I suppose all share a common destruction now. There were groups of French officers in the long gallery, and we gravely saluted each other as we passed. From the Town Hall I went to the Cathedral of St. Martin, which was also in pathetic process of restoration.

Inside that big building everything was very quiet and solemn. There were a few soldiers, French, Belgian, and English moving about. I did not know at that time that the tomb of Jansenius was there, or I should have looked for it. There is another fine church in Ypres, St. James's, I think. As I returned from this church, I saw many French *cuirassiers* in the Place d'Armes, making a brave show, with their long horsehair plumes and burnished breast-plates.

51

Outside our Headquarters I saw a crowd of British soldiers around what appeared to be two Belgian civilians. I stopped to hear what was going on, and my ears were saluted with as rich a brogue as ever came out of Tipperary. The "Belgian peasants" turned out to be two men of my regiment who had been taken prisoners at Mons, but who had managed shortly afterwards to escape. From then till now they had been wandering about the country, hiding in woods, the bottom of wells, etc., and befriended all through by the French and Belgian people, though to harbour them was death.

At one time they had been given a lift in a "gentleman's motorcar," they told me. After weeks of wandering, during which time, of course, they had been given up for dead, they had got into the vicinity of Ypres, and hearing that there were British troops there they had come in. Their adventures would have filled a book. It was a piece of luck for them to meet an officer of their own regiment. I gave them a good dinner, some money, tobacco and pipes, and wrote home to the depot about them, to relieve their people's anxiety.

One of them was called Murphy, and he came from Enniscorthy. The other was a native of Kilkenny. Poor fellows, they had suffered enough, and I am thankful they escaped the horrors that were in store for us, for I heard that they were to be sent home at once to refit.

I slept that night in a little house with a winding staircase leading up to my room—a typical house of the Middle Ages. On the morrow we were to turn and move eastwards from Ypres, to confront the enemy.

We started very early on the 16th October, long before it was light, and I moved with Headquarters to where the ancient battlements are, and the moat. Again, there was the confusion that seems inseparable from night movements through towns, and my general's anxiety and impatience were most acute. In the end, however, the tangle got straightened out, and we pushed on. But Headquarters only proceeded as far as a little inn at a point quite near the city, where the railway crossed the road, while the troops went forward to take up positions that were to become historic.

Of the 15,000 splendid infantry that marched jauntily out from Ypres that day, a bare 2,000 were to escape death, wounds, or captivity, and of 400 officers scarcely 40.

From that date to the day I was wounded, on the 2nd November, events crowded so thick and fast upon one another that to write a connected account of what happened would be impossible to one who played only a very subordinate part in them.

I must say a word, though, of what was the manner of poor Tom Condon's death. After I had been carried in by two brave fellows of the 60th, and was about to depart from our Headquarters in the Huize Beukenhorst to hospital in Ypres, Tom came to me to say goodbye. I felt dreadfully leaving him behind, and I asked him whether he would like me to try to get him home.

"Ah, sure," he said, "I'll see it out."

Some weeks afterwards, when in Guy's Hospital, I wrote to his father at Clonmel to ask for news of Tom. He told me that Tom had been killed on the night of the 5th of November by a shell. (Or, rather, with the wonderful delicacy of that class of Irishman, he wrote it to my nurse, for communication to me—Author.)

I afterwards heard the hour, and it corresponded with the moment of my operation on board the hospital ship that brought me home. I had written down in my notebook the few words that the surgeon told me I had spoken when under chloroform. They were:—

"You stop here, Tom, while I ride forward with the general."

Poor fellow, I had always striven to keep him as far as possible out of danger, only to have him killed in my absence.

My servant was with him to the end. He wrote that Tom was in a stable with the horses when it happened, and that he did not suffer much.

★★★★★★

We remained at the inn nearly all that day. The road was greatly congested with our transport and with the men of the 87th (French) Territorial Division, which had come up to support us. No further British troops could be heard of as being within reach of us. I think it was put in orders next morning that our division had come into line with the remainder of the Expeditionary Force, and that British troops were now on our right and left. No doubt they were, but we received no direct support until the 24th (this being the 16th), when our line had been badly broken, and matters were looking desperate.

While we were at the inn a Belgian armoured-car, which was attached to our division, brought in a captured *Uhlan*. This car was commanded by a little bearded man, whom I mentally christened "The Gnome," and who never went out without bagging at least one prisoner. The number of Germans he killed was considerable. The prisoner whom he brought in on this occasion was given exactly the same food and drink as we had, and later on sent into Ypres hospital in a motorcar. Off another *Uhlan* prisoner I secured a wonderful map of Northern France and Belgium, all covered over with tiny conventional signs (for wells, forges, barns, etc., etc.), showing how thoroughly prepared the Germans were for this campaign.

"The Gnome" was clad from head to foot in black oilskins, and wore a sou'-wester hat. He knew no English, and not much French, and his pluck and disregard, for danger were amazing. With him was a callow British subaltern, as unlike him as possible, and a chauffeur who dwelt in the bottom of the car, and knew his business very well.

I was to have a ride on that car that night, and the manner of its happening was this:

While we were yet at the inn it was reported to me that certain Mess stores were required from Ypres. I took one of the motors in for them, and when I returned, I found that our Headquarters had been shifted. I knew that they were to be established that night in one of the numerous *châteaux* on the Ypres-Menin road, but which of them exactly I did not know. So, when I had come racing back in the dark and enquired of a sentry at the gate of the first one whether it housed Divisional Headquarters, having received an answer in the affirmative, I went in. The *château* was occupied by Headquarters, right enough, but they were those of an Artillery Brigade (Donald F——was one of the officers). I had incautiously omitted to tell the chauffeur to wait, and when I came out again, he was gone.

So, there was nothing for it but to walk. I had on a heavy greatcoat (for the night was bitterly cold), and had furthermore to carry the box of Mess stores which I had procured in Ypres. F—— lent me his soldier servant, and off we trudged along the dark, muddy road. After we had gone about three-quarters of a mile two very bright lights hove into view far down the road, coming towards us. I stood in the middle of the road and hailed them. It turned out to be the Belgian armoured-car containing "The Gnome," the driver, and the British subaltern. They were making their way back to the inn, thinking that our Headquarters were still where they had left them. I told them that these had moved on to some *château* on the side of the road, and that we might as well all go on together. Then, having thanked and dismissed the servant who had helped me, I climbed up into the car and sat perched on top of one of its heavily-armoured sides. The driver (who was in a sort of well at my feet—I remember that I stood on him once) brought the car round with some difficulty, and off we went.

It was rather eerie work going along in this strange and deadly contraption in the black darkness. At every few paces a sentry would step out from the side of the road and challenge us. And we had to pull up, too, at every challenge, or be quite certainly fired on at close quarters. Several unfortunate officers and motorcycle dispatch riders were killed in this way by their own side—men who could ill be spared.

We had to cruise up and down the road several times before we could find the place. All these *châteaux* stood well back from the road, and were hidden by trees. But at last we saw the red and green lamp that marked Divisional Headquarters, and we entered. The *château* turned out to be a large square modern house, in which everything was very new and on a generous scale. It had been left by its owners "all standing," and the Germans, who had been there quite recently and at the time of their advance on Paris, had drunk the cellars dry and scattered the broken bottles all over the entrance steps and hall.

I shared a room at the top of the house with our veterinary officer, and, except for a few nights when we changed our Headquarters to a *château* nearer still to the enemy, or which I spent out, I slept there every night that circumstances permitted.

There must have been some thirty officers and as many clerks quartered in that house, while downstairs in the basement were many servants, cooks, men on guard, etc. The house, as I have said, was very new. It was heated by hot-water pipes, the secret of the manipulation of which we soon discovered, and it was lit by incandescent gas which was worked by a small motor underneath the stables and garage. These were about forty yards from the house. Another small gas-engine pumped up water, until the Belgian caretaker (who had stuck to his post when the family had left) fled, terrified by the shells that kept exploding all around us. In every bedroom were a holy-water font and statue of Our Lady, and all up the main staircase were photographs of the various stages in the building and completion of the house, down to a pathetic group of the housewarming party, which included a stately ecclesiastic, who, presumably, had given it his blessing.

In the morning, when I was able to take note of the exterior, I saw that the *château* must have replaced an older building, for there were two fine rows of old trees leading away from it in the rear, whereas only quite young saplings were planted in its front. The big forest that lies about five kilometres to the east of Ypres (the *château* was at the fifth kilometre stone) enclosed it on two sides. It faced north, and in front of it were a small rose-garden and paddock, while behind it there were pleasure grounds, terminating in a well-stocked flower and vegetable garden. In the latter I found some lovely violets, a few of which I picked and enclosed in a letter home. The *château* was called the "Huize Beukenhorst," and was just to the east of the little black-and-white village of Hooge. It was said that the wife of the owner was a daughter of the German Chancellor, and that for that reason the German artillery would not fire on it.

Whether it was owing to this, or because it was not marked on the Ordnance maps (even the spy one which I had captured), I do not know, but the fact remains that up to the very end of October, although many shells fell in the grounds, not one struck the house. A poor fellow was cut in two almost outside the door one day soon after our arrival, and splinters of the shell fell amongst a crowd of us who were on the steps, but up to the day I left only about three shells had struck the walls, doing little damage. By now, I suppose, it is a heap of ruins.

★★★★★★

It must be remembered that this was written in January, 1915. Few will recognise "Stirling Castle" under the name given to it in these pages, which was taken from a picture-postcard of the house found *in situ*—Author.)

★★★★★★

I do not recollect anything very important taking place on the 17th of October, but that night we received instructions resulting in an order which began:

The division will advance tomorrow and take Menin. . . .

There were very large bodies of the enemy advancing upon us from the north-east, Menin lay about south-east by east, was reported to be (together with Wervicq) strongly held, and we should have to move without support across the enemy's line of advance. The 87th Division of French Territorials had certainly dug a line of trenches in our rear, but this was not a division intended at the time for offensive warfare.

However, the movement was ordered for the morning of Sunday, 18th, to start at about 8 a.m. I had heard overnight from one of the clerks that the only Catholic chaplain with the division was to say Mass at six the next morning in a house about half-a-mile farther along the road. This was the Rev. Father M——, whom I had known in 1904 at Middelburg, Transvaal, where he was our Regimental Chaplain.

When, at about a quarter to six the next morning, I got to the house indicated, I found a handful of R.A.M.C. men as congregation (it was the 22nd Field Ambulance's billet).

In what had probably been the drawing-room of this little country-house in the wood of Veldhoek, Mass was celebrated. There were two of these houses in the wood, on opposite sides of the road, this one standing on the right, or south, side of the road from Ypres to Menin. Most of the furniture had been removed, and only a few English and American sporting prints were left on the walls. These were of the rather silly type, depicting lanky Yankees driving impossible trotting horses, and smoking long cigars the while. Negro servants in attendance, and tiny jockeys being ordered by grim trainers to stand no nonsense from viciously kicking race-horses.

CHAPTER 7

The Offensive-Defensive

At about 8 o'clock the forward movement ("to take Menin") began. We turned off from the main road, in what was then the pretty little village of Gheluvelt. To my mind now it presents a ghastly picture of a shell-riven place of ruin, and of dead men and horses. Time after time during the next fortnight it was heavily shelled by the Germans, as they slowly pressed us back. But on this 18th October, it was still out of their range, and as we rode through it its single street was full of people and its church, so soon to be knocked to pieces, was crowded with worshippers. Its windmill was to remain intact long after almost every house had fallen, until it, too, shared the common fate.

We only got as far as the hamlet of Pozelhoek, where we received orders to halt, and after a wearisome wait, during which we heard the guns thundering in the direction of Becelaere and Passchendaele, to the north, Sir Henry Rawlinson and his staff arrived by motor and had a confabulation with my general. As a result, we never moved our Headquarters a step nearer to the enemy, but instead we were to be back again that very evening in the Château Beukenhorst, at Hooge.

The tide of war was now rolling southward and westward, and the road was soon crowded with refugees from the villages lying along our front.

It was desperately pathetic to see them. Entire families passed us, each one forming its own particular little group. There was generally a large country-cart, drawn by a yoke of oxen. In it would be the youngest children of the family, often chortling with joy at the novel experience, it being the first day's journey, and the pinch of hunger and fatigue not yet felt. We could see their jolly little faces appearing over the sides of the lumbering vehicle. Then would come the elder children and the mothers, on foot, with their eyes full of terror. And then a tiny cart or two, drawn by panting dogs, with the poor old grannies sitting in them, bolt upright, and maintaining a sort of senile dignity. They reminded me of the old people driving in their ass-carts to Mass on Sundays at home.

After a long delay in the little inn, where we had fixed our headquarters, the general said he would go forward in the motor to a ridge near the hamlet of Terhand to reconnoitre. I—— and I went with him, and from the top of the ridge we had a fine view of the country to the north and north-east. It was more undulating than the ground immediately round Ypres, which was flat and monotonous. The usual style of thing in Western Flanders is a level countryside, closely cultivated, and dotted with thick, well-kept woods. Pollarded willows grow in lines between the fields, and along the numerous drains and where the roads run there are invariably poplars, as in France. But from the Terhand ridge as we looked north-east, the view was far more diversified and interesting. Large villages, with fine church spires, could be seen on low-wooded ridges, and now over Passchendaele and Moorslede we saw the shrapnel bursting, and great columns of smoke rising to the sky.

We left the car under some cover and went on foot to get a better view. Near us was a regiment entrenched (I think the Scots Fusiliers), and a couple of batteries, very cunningly concealed, and firing at long range. The infantry trenches were well dug, but not particularly well hidden. I noticed some Belgian peasants manfully helping our men with the digging. The bursting shrapnel looked strangely beautiful— at a distance; strings of puffs of white smoke high above the ground. Very soon we were to know what the lash of those strings was like. After a careful survey of the position, and noting how strongly the enemy's attack was developing beyond our left flank, we returned to the motor, and sped back to our headquarters. But I——, who had reconnoitred the road previously, made a mistake at a certain turning, and we found ourselves on a very sandy by-road, and were compelled to go a couple of miles out of our way before we regained the high-road. By this time the general's temper had not improved.

Our forces were already falling back when we returned to our inn, and after a while Headquarters were actually in front of their own troops. The general and the rest of the staff departed in the end in a great hurry, and I found myself left behind with his escort of a troop of the Northumberland Hussars, various motorcars and grooms, and a signal-waggon. It was beginning to grow dark when I put myself at the head of these and retired, too. My mare, "Dawn," had gone very lame, and I had to change on to "Sportsman." When I arrived back at the Château Beukenhorst I found things re-established just as we had left them that morning. The "taking of Menin" had not materialised!

(Afterwards, when in hospital in London, I heard from a Highland officer who was in it that three of our battalions had actually approached Menin, and that had the Gordons gone on a little farther they would inevitably have been cut off.)

On the 19th I find nothing recorded in my book, except that I motored into Ypres to buy wine for the mess—six bottles of *Vin Ordinaire* at two *francs* the bottle; and very good it was.

On the 20th a "reconnaissance in force" was ordered to be carried out by our 21st (?) Brigade on the left (north) of the Ypres-Menin road. It was recalled, after it had suffered heavy loss. The enemy was now shelling the grounds of our *château*, and causing several casualties.

On the 21st the enemy had advanced from the north-east and east, and was in possession of the Terhand Ridge, and shelling Gheluvelt and Veldhoek. I rode with a message to the 21st Brigade Headquarters, and on my way was handed an unexploded incendiary bomb by a man of the Scots Guards. He had found it stuck into a hole in a house in Veldhoek.

It was either this day or the next (my "diary" is very empty about now) that I was told by the general to fetch the Northumberland Hussars from Hooge Château and put them in the firing line, just to the east of Veldhoek, where the pressure had become acute. I rode off and got them, and with their second-in-command and K——, their adjutant (whom I had known in India), I took them to a spot on the road where they could dismount under cover and conceal their horses. I remember how hard it was going along that shelled road to keep from trotting out too fast. In fact, we three officers got a couple of hundred yards in front of the troopers at one point, and had to pull up to await them. I admired them very much. They never departed on that occasion from a calm jog-trot, such as one employs hunting, going from cover to cover. Many of them were, in fact, hunt-servants. In this campaign they proved most admirable soldiers, and goodness knows they were highly tried. Nothing seemed to come amiss to them, and they were placed at everybody's beck and call.

By the evening of the 21st matters had begun to look serious, and, as a precautionary measure, the Divisional Transport had been sent back to a point to the south of Ypres. But at about 4.30 p.m. the gen-

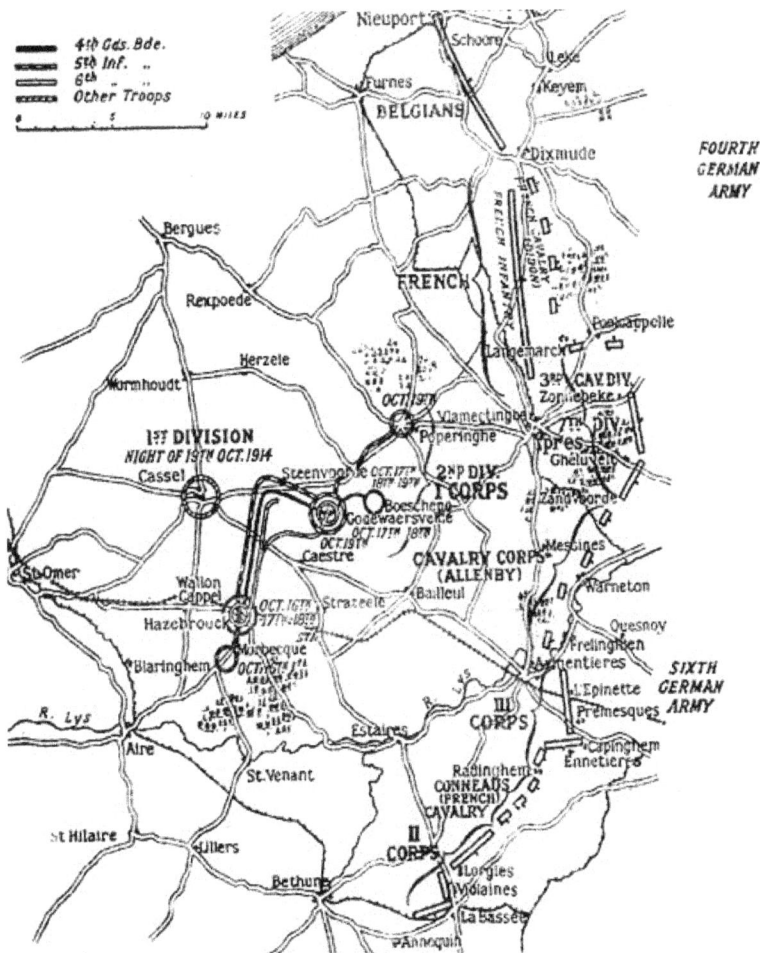

LOCATIONS OF THE ALLIED AND GERMAN ARMIES, 19TH OCTOBER, 1914

eral sent me in a motorcar to stop it, and to tell H—— or D—— to send all that was essential to units back to the spot where it had outspanned the previous night. I accordingly set off, and passed through Zillebeke. The road beyond that village was choked with cavalry and transport. I met the 10th Hussars again. Poor D—— , who had worked frightfully hard to get the transport away, was much put out at the idea of having to bring it all back again. It was now 5 o'clock; he said he would get it done by 8.

I met the Duke of Westminster, who seemed to spend his time carrying dispatches between Ypres and London. He told me he had left London at 9 o'clock the previous night, and arrived at Poperinghe (the then railhead) at eight that morning—pretty good going!

That night the enemy pitched his shells all around the *château*, but none actually struck it. It was some days before we learnt to distinguish absolutely between shells that were being fired from our side and those that were bursting near us from the enemy. Personally, I found it a great help not to know for certain! One used to hear officers enquiring from those in the artillery whether any particularly startling report was "an arrival or a departure," and the phrase was rather a happy one. Generally, the bursting ones would be preceded by a shrill, whirring noise, or a shell would seem to be almost *sauntering* overhead, with exactly the noise (though intensified) that a stone makes when thrown along a sheet of ice. The big "Black Marias" always went to ground in fours, with a horrid noise that was like a cough, or it sounded like "*Wump*" said very loud. Every night now was to be disturbed by the sound of heavy rifle fire, in long bursts.

At daybreak on the 22nd I rode with the general and K—— to Zonnebeke, which was the left of our line, held by the Welsh Fusiliers, of the 22nd Brigade. Tom came with me. The brigade had been very heavily attacked during the night, and had suffered many casualties. My general had had long and earnest confabulations with Brigadier-General L—— on the telephone all through the night. I heard afterwards that the movement of one body had had to be held up in the streets of Zonnebeke for a considerable time in order to enable General L—— to reply to my general's queries, his end of the wire being in the middle of all the turmoil. "Stick it out! You *must* hold on: there can be no question of anything else," was the sort of thing that went from our end many times during the next few days and to all three brigades. And they, for their part, needed little urging.

We got to Zonnebeke *via* a tiny hamlet called Eksternest, and when we reached it, we found our infantry falling back to dig a rearward line of trenches in the grey light of morning. The Welsh Fusiliers had had heavy losses, and among the killed was young Snead-Cox. Poor lad, his father had asked me to "keep a friendly eye on him"! The general left me with the horses, while we went on to interview General L——.

The enemy pressed our line hard all that day, and was beginning to close in on Gheluvelt in the centre of our position. Colonel P—— (our A. A. and Q.M.G.), Colonel Sir Frederick Ponsonby, and de B—— (our French liaison officer) were returning from a "joy-ride" to that village about noon, when a shell exploded on the road quite close to them. It wounded P—— in the leg, and Sir Frederick Ponsonby's horse was hit in the neck.

On the 23rd our Headquarters were still at the Château Beukenhorst. I had many messages to deliver that day, mostly to the 21st Brigade, between Veldhoek and Gheluvelt. When I took the first one, I did not know that Brigade Headquarters had shifted back, and were not in so advanced a position as they had been when I had taken other messages there the day before. I was making for the cottage in which they had been established when I saw that shells were falling all around it, and that it was deserted. Seeing my mistake, I cast back a bit, and eventually discovered the right place.

Our position was now this: the 22nd Brigade, on the left, still clung to the ridge of Zonnebeke; the 21st, in the centre, was entrenched just west of Gheluvelt; the 20th had its centre at Kruisseik. The German pressure was becoming very pronounced, and they seemed to have unlimited troops to hurl against us. I had now a great deal of riding and motoring to do to various parts of our line, and to the cavalry. Once I had to go to General Byng, commanding the 3rd Cavalry Division, at Zillebeke, to ask him if "C" Battery was available to fire in the direction of America, the queerly-named little village to the south-east from whence our position was being severely shelled. I was to find out whether the point of junction between our right (the Gordons) and the cavalry was a certain stream near Hollebeke, and to say that Brigadier-General R——B—— had complained that many German snipers had taken up their post in the gap between Zandvoorde and Kruiseik, causing him heavy loss.

We had been anxiously awaiting news of the 1st and 2nd Infantry Divisions, which were said to have been coming up on our right and left respectively in support; but so far there had been no sign of them.

I was to tell General Byng that he *might* receive some support from portions of the Second Division, but that he was not to count on it. I performed my mission successfully, but I had to make two more visits to General Byng that day. For the second of these I took a small open car, my horses being tired. The driver seemed to relish the work hugely. A shell burst thirty yards from it while he was waiting for me outside Byng's Headquarters, and only seemed to have amused him. "C" Battery was already in action, and not available, therefore, to take on America. The 106th Battery was also not available. General Byng asked me to try to get General Rawlinson to arrange for the armoured-train to do the job. I met an old Murree friend of mine at the Cavalry Headquarters, in Johnny B———. He was A.D.C. to General Byng.

As we motored back through Zillebeke the sky was full of aeroplanes, both ours and Taubes. Our men were firing with perfect impartiality on both. Beyond Zonnebeke the Germans had sent up a sausage-shaped captive balloon for fire-direction purposes. I could see the puffs of smoke from our shrapnel all around it, but it was not touched. A little farther on along the road I stopped the car in order to watch two of our biplanes chase a Taube out of the sky, and as I did so a stout man in civilian clothes passed me on foot, going in the direction of Ypres. I afterwards found out that he was the Baron de Something-or-other, and that he had just left his *château*, which was the one in Hooge, and to which I had often repaired with my general to interview Sir Henry Rawlinson. Very shortly after the owner had left it the enemy plumped a couple of 11-inch shells clean into it, killing or wounding a crowd of staff officers, among whom was Colonel Percival. The night before this occurred, I had been sitting with them all in the very room that was afterwards wrecked by the shells.

It was said that the baron had been in communication with the Germans all the time, and that they knew when he had left the house. If this was so, it must have been a bitter blow to him to know that it was no longer to be allowed to escape, for it was a beautiful house, richly and tastefully furnished, and his studio (he was an artist) was full of clever pictures. Of course, he may not have been a spy at all, but it was curious that he should have remained on in his home so long after all the other inhabitants of the district had gone, and also that his departure should have taken place just before the house was shelled. To people at home this spy business must sound a bit overdone, but it was such an unpleasant reality "out there" that soldiers might have been excused if it got a bit on their nerves.

It was most distressing to have to realise that spies—indigenous ones—were everywhere. Brave and wonderful as the Belgians had been all through the time of their trials, it was none the less true that there were many, many black sheep among them. I have heard it stated that it was so in France, too. Perhaps it would be the same in England. It seems to be all a question of Germany having thought it worthwhile to salt the ground over which she meant to fight.

Many were the devices of the spies, and the simple, straightforward, "playing the game" British officer was the last person in the world to cope with them. But he learnt to do it in course of time, though severe enough measures were seldom taken; at least that is my impression.

The underground telephone wire, the windmill, and the carrier-pigeon were the systems that I came in contact with personally. In the first the wires had evidently been laid down a considerable time before we came along, and we knew that the Germans had been over all this ground in their great sweeping movement upon Paris. I often saw our sappers digging for buried wire along the Ypres-Menin road, between the 23rd and 31st of October. It was supposed that the receivers were hidden in lofts, haystacks, etc., but I never heard of one being discovered. Sometimes even we ourselves had left the ordinary telegraph wire standing along the roadside.

About the 21st October, after dark, our transport was feeling its way from Ypres to a spot on the Menin road whence it could supply the firing line. It had got as far as Hooge (where the Baron's *château* was) when it came under shell fire which obliged it to halt. After a bit the shelling ceased and the convoy started to move on again. Immediately the shells came at it again from seven or eight miles away, and after that whenever it halted the shelling ceased and whenever it tried to move on it started again. Noise could hardly have given it away, for it made very little, and there was far too much other noise going on all the time.

As regards windmills. The idea was that the sails were made to revolve according to a preconcerted plan, whenever a large body of troops came abreast of the mill. This was, of course, a daytime dodge. It was first worked on two companies of the Bedfords about the 21st October. The day was perfectly still, and as the centre of the two companies came opposite to a windmill at Gheluvelt the sails suddenly made a half-turn, and immediately a storm of shrapnel burst over the main street, knocking out many of the men. We heard, too, of tricks being worked on much the same principle with the hands of clocks, but I never heard of any definite instance of this.

On the occasion I have mentioned, however, the miller was caught in his mill and brought to our headquarters by a party of intensely aggrieved Bedfords. He loudly protested his innocence and sobbed bitterly, declaring that he had given our men food and accepted no payment, and that when the Germans had passed that way, he had given them nothing. I don't know what became of him, but I hoped that if he was innocent, he might be spared, and that if he was shot, he might have been guilty. All this sort of work is hateful, and the thought that we might have been killing a well-disposed peasant who, out of his tiny store had given freely to our men, was utterly repugnant. The Germans would have shot him out of hand on the merest suspicion.

Carrier-pigeons were used over and over again, and peasants were frequently discovered with them concealed under their clothing. One day I saw a pigeon go up from the middle of a wood just east of our Headquarters. He went straight up in the approved homing way, made a few circles, and then darted off towards the German lines. The Master of Belhaven, who was our intelligence officer, happened to be standing near me, and I told him what I had seen. We decided to "draw" the wood there and then. It was divided by rides, and the portion which we meant to search was about 100 yards by 60.

As we started off, I saw three or four men of the Grenadier Guards wandering towards our headquarters. They had lost their way, they said. So, I fell them in, and told them to "bring on "the wood, just as beaters would do in covert shooting. They extended, and started to advance, while B—— and I, with drawn revolvers, posted ourselves at the opposite corners. I remember noticing how the shrapnel scarred the tree-trunks, making deep continuous marks down the bark like those caused by lightning. After a bit the stalkers emerged on our side of the wood, without result.

So, we gave it up. But an hour afterwards I happened to be in the same spot, and caught sight of a party of *five* peasants, stealing out from that very wood. I sent some men in pursuit, and they captured the party. There were three men and two women. We searched the men, and they had no pigeons concealed about them. Nobody proposed to search the women, and probably these had none either. They all loudly protested that they had only come back to see if anything was left of their farms, and that they had hid in the wood by day. Here again came in the bewildering question of how to distinguish between a cunning liar and a piteous, simple-minded peasant. Unless a man was taken absolutely red-handed, I am sure we never punished him. But then among real spies we must have been a by-word for incompetent leniency.

Two spy experiences are the following, though we were never quite certain that either case was really one of spying. The first occurred on the morning we left Ypres, to march against the enemy. As the members of our Staff were preparing to move off tightening girths, etc. a small group of French officers came trotting across the Place in the semi-darkness, and drew rein opposite to our Headquarters. They were a *chef-de-bataillon*, a captain and a lieutenant. They said they had been sent on from the 87th French Territorial Division (which was coming up to support us), and that they wished to know what our immediate movements were to be, in order that they might report to their general.

They seemed typical French officers, smart and well-groomed; but I remembered afterwards that they only addressed themselves to some young officers who were, for one reason or another, attached to our staff. From these they could not have got much information, but they clattered off, with many punctilious salutes, by the way they had come. When, later on, we met the staff of the 87th French Division they assured us that no officers had gone forward from them—at least with their knowledge.

The second case occurred much later on, and I only heard of it long afterwards in hospital, from an officer in the Gordon Highlanders. He told me that in the middle of the most desperate fighting—I think it was on the 1st November (so that I am anticipating a little)—an officer in British staff uniform rode up to his regiment (the Gordons) and ordered them to retire. It was a most critical moment, and the retirement, which was begun at once, must have had grave consequences, had not the brigadier-general, or someone else in authority, ordered the men back into their trenches.

The staff officer who gave the order was never traced.

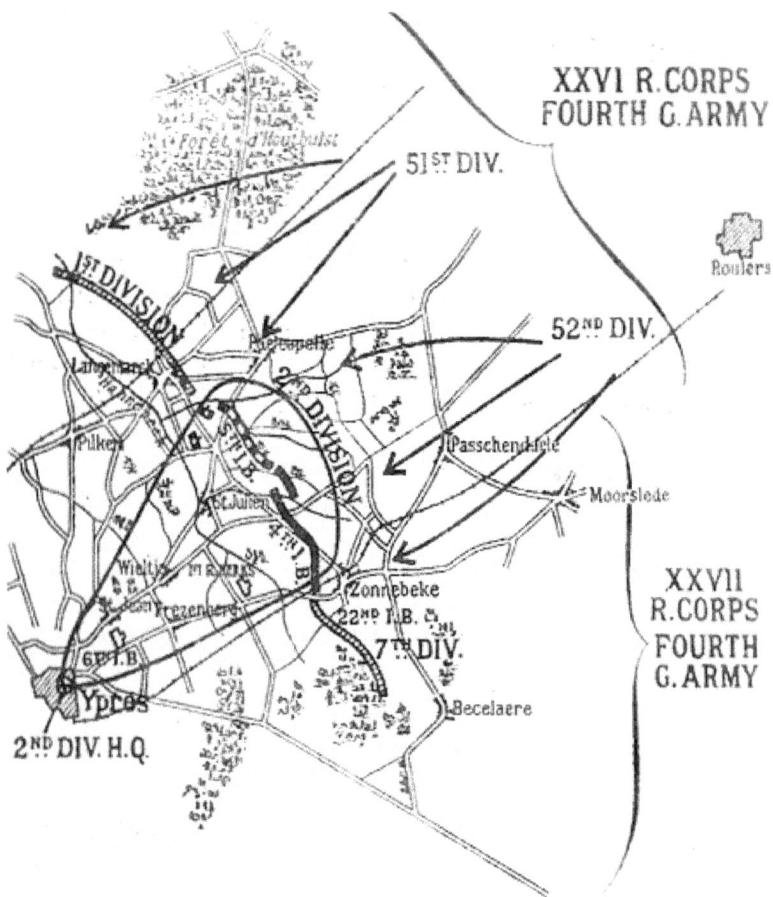

XXVI R.CORPS
FOURTH G.ARMY

51ST DIV.

Roulers

1ST DIVISION

52ND DIV.

Langemarck

2ND DIVISION

Passchendaele

Pilken

Moorslede

St Julien

XXVII
R.CORPS
FOURTH
G.ARMY

Wieltje

Frezenberg

Zonnebeke

22ND I.B.

7TH DIV.

6TH I.B.

Ypres

Becelaere

2ND DIV. H.Q.

Reference 2ND DIV.
4TH (Guards) Bde.
5TH Inf. Bde.
6TH " "
1ST & 7TH Div.

MENIN

Wervicq

BATTLE OF LANGEMARK, FROM 21ST–24TH OCTOBER, 1914

CHAPTER 8

Hot Work

To return to my narrative. The 24th October was a very anxious day, and from now onward things began to work themselves up into a *crescendo* of anxiety and fierce fighting against odds. On the previous day, the 23rd, our regiments, who were holding a 9-mile front against the continuous assaults of overwhelming forces of the enemy, had all suffered severely. In particular the Wiltshires (21st Brigade, in the centre) had lost enormously, and had ceased to exist as a unit.

At about 7 o'clock that night a young subaltern of that regiment had arrived at our Headquarters. He was starving, and yet almost unable to keep awake. He told us that his section of trench had been completely filled in by German shells, and that he had only managed to extricate himself with the greatest difficulty, and that he had been unable to find more than a dozen or so men of his regiment who had survived the German attacks. So great had been the concussion of the shells that both his wrist-watches had stopped. It was his first experience of war, and he told me that the very first thing that had happened when he got into his trench was that the man next him had had his head blown off.

We gave the poor young fellow some food, and I don't know what afterwards happened to him.

During one of my visits to Brigadier-General W——'s (21st Brigade) Headquarters that day I came in for a view of a terrific artillery duel between the Germans south-east of Gheluvelt and our batteries about Zillebeke. It was getting on towards dark, and the sky, besides being red with the glow from burning houses and farmsteads, was crossed and re-crossed by the fire and smoke of shells. With the brigadier-general I went out into a field to watch. The duel was going on right across us, as it were, at no great distance; but our own portion of the front was for the moment quiet. The noise was terrific. Gun seemed to answer gun, shot for shot, and it was as though all other fighting had come to a sudden stop while the big pieces settled their differences for themselves.

Well, on the morning of the 24th the reports that reached us from our three brigades were of a very serious nature. The enemy's artillery had got the range of their trenches to a nicety, and unless our guns could locate their batteries and give our infantry some help the line could not hold out. My diary under this date says:

> Gunners very anxious about non-location of enemy's guns. Is there one mounted on a tramline?

The gunners were beginning to suspect that the Germans were continually shifting their gun-emplacements, in the manner here suggested, so as to render the task of locating them more difficult.

Our signalling officer had a powerful telescope, which he had mounted in one of the upstairs rooms of the Huize Beukenhorst, looking northeast. Through it we could see fields strewn with German dead, right away beyond Zonnebeke, and in the direction of Dadizeele. I had not much time for looking through it, however, for many were the errands I was sent upon that day.

At last there had been tangible evidence of reinforcements reaching us. The Irish Guards had come up on our left, beyond Zonnebeke, where there was desperate fighting. I heard that there had been some misunderstanding with regard to defining the responsibility for the defence of the railway station at Zonnebeke. At all events, the enemy took the station, and badly enfiladed one of our regiments, the Queen's. There was talk, too, of reinforcements from the 2nd Division reaching our centre, by the road from Ypres. *That* was how we wanted them— *through* and *with* us, not on a flank while our line was being smashed!

At one time during that morning of the 24th things were indeed so bad that we sent all our baggage away, and began to fear that the whole divisional staff would be captured or destroyed. As far as I remember, it was about midday when we heard that our centre (immediately ahead of us) had been broken, and that the Germans were surging through along the road. The general sent for me, and told me that he put the defence of himself and his staff into my hands, that I was to reconnoitre the pleasure-grounds of the *château* for a defensive position, and that I was to collect every available man—clerk, groom, chauffeur, etc.—who could hold a rifle, and defend Headquarters to

LANGEMARK

the last.

I accordingly fell in every odd man I saw, and with the Headquarters troop of Northumberland Hussars as a very welcome stiffening, they came to about forty all told. I selected a line just outside the grounds, to the east, where a slight embankment at the side of a road offered a certain amount of ready-made cover. I divided the men up into squads, each under an N.C.O., and told them that on my giving the word, they were to make, in skirmishing order, for the positions I had indicated.

Just as I had arranged all this along came G——, and he told me he thought it would be much better if the men were to occupy the top storey of the *château*, whence they could fire on any of the enemy that might attempt to pass it on either side. The general happened to hear of the proposed change, and told me that he had entrusted the job to me, and meant me to carry it out.

That settled it, and at that moment a pretty considerable body of our infantry came stumbling back along the road. Word was passed that the enemy was hard on their traces. I gave the signal, and my command took up its station. Young N——, the officer in command of the Headquarters troop, came to help me, and I was very glad of his assistance. I served out wire-cutters to the N.C.O.'s so that when the general and staff had got away, they might cut the wires behind them and allow their men to get back. I cut a judicious strand here and there myself; and we settled down to await the foe.

It was a motley crew that I had under my orders, and my loudly-put question "Is there any man here who has never fired a rifle before?" though it rather gave offence to the hussars (who fancied themselves) was not altogether misplaced, for one or two of the specially-enlisted chauffeurs and clerks undoubtedly never had. My excellent cook, Vincent, the funny man of the piece throughout this campaign, and oftentimes both my despair and my consolation, informed me in best Cockney that he had never fired outside a shooting gallery, at bottles; whereat those who lay nearest to him in the ditch laughed. It was then I remembered having heard him boasting to a soldier, some time before, that he had won "the M—— Cup" for shooting. I couldn't help reminding him of the fact now.

"I 'ad to put that young fellow in 'is place, Sir," he said.

Our chief of the staff was a Colonel M——, and I've no doubt the cook invented the "cup" on the spot, thinking he was listening.

Our position ran at right angles to the road from Ypres, the road being to the left of it. In front of us there was about four hundred yards of open ground, and beyond that was the thick belt of wood which I have referred to elsewhere. The road ran through the centre of this wood, right opposite to us. Either the enemy would, if he came at all, come crowding down the road, in which case we would give him beans the instant he emerged, or he would line the edge of the wood, and start firing on us. I told my men to lie very low and wait.

One or two of them were Wiltshires, but lately come from their truly terrible ordeal. They had lined out with the rest, but in truth there was little use in their doing so, for their rifles had, in one way or another, become quite useless. I saw my excellent servant, Weekes, whom I knew to be a marksman, lying down very business-like and cool. Many as were the queer places in which he had seen me, I don't think there was ever one to beat this. I do hope that he is still alive, and that someday we shall be able to laugh over the experience. Not that I have ever known Weekes to laugh. But still he *might!*

While we were waiting there, I—— had been sent hot-foot, just as I had been a few days before, to fetch the Northumberland Hussars, and to put them into a gap in the trenches. This he did most admirably, I afterwards heard. He conducted them to a certain point, and then dismounted and took them forward. In doing so he was shot in the arm. K——, their adjutant, was shot in the chest and hand; and together they were brought back to Headquarters. The Germans were now pouring through the gap in our centre, and we ourselves were momentarily expecting to have to open fire, when a battalion of the long-expected 2nd Division (I think it was the Connaught Rangers) advanced up the road, and the immediate tension was relieved.

After a time, I was able to dismiss my men, and report all clear. I was immediately given instructions as to a personal reconnaissance. I was to find Col. W——, commanding the newly come up 5th Brigade. Very heavy fighting had been taking place all day in the woods east of Eksternest ("Eagles' Nest," my general called it) and north of Veldhoek. Telephonic communication had gone by the board, and we did not know what the situation was like over there. Our 22nd Brigade, to his left, or what was left of it, was to be withdrawn and brought into reserve just north of Veldhoek. Our 21st Brigade was all jumbled up with W——'s reinforcements.

My orders were to find out from this officer what was the exact situation in the wood in front of him, whether he was in direct communication with the units of his command, and whether he was going to advance on the right of the 6th Brigade, which we knew to be intact.

I had to go to Colonel W——'s Headquarters three times within an hour, and I rode each of my three chargers in succession. "Brightness" went best that day, and the bursting of the shells made her go "16-*annas*," too.

The 5th Brigade Headquarters were in a little, isolated farmhouse, with cultivated land all around it, and to the west of the dense belt of wood in which all the carnage was taking place. I found that Col. W—— was in direct communication with his own regiment, the gallant Worcesters, but with regard to the others, communication had broken down. After getting all the information I could from him, I galloped on towards the belt of wood, and as I got to it I met Brigadier-General L——, at the head of part of his brigade, the Queen's. They were moving along on the outskirts of the wood, going due south, to take up their allotted position near Veldhoek. Shortly before I had met the handful of men that remained of the Welsh Fusiliers, also moving to Veldhoek, and headed by their Colonel, Cadogan, who was almost the only officer with them.

I spoke for some time with General L——, and from him I was able to discover the dispositions of the relieving regiments in the wood. From him I learnt that one of his battalions, the Warwicks, had been fired on for hours by a relieving regiment. The Warwicks had behaved all through with the utmost gallantry, and this last trial was too dreadful. Their colonel, Loring, was among the many killed that day. Struck in the foot by a shrapnel bullet, he had nevertheless refused to go to the dressing station, and a rifle bullet shortly afterwards ended his splendid career.

General L—— told me that the reinforcements had only just arrived in time; and with the information that he had given me I returned finally to my general.

As I rode back my route led me past a battery of our 4.7 guns that was concealed in a sandy, sunken track near Eksternest. Late that night I was awakened by rifle shots, the noise of which seemed to come from near this battery. Thinking that this might mean that snipers had crept up to within easy shooting distance of the gunners (the big guns always went on firing, at intervals, all through the night) I went downstairs at about 2 a.m. and woke up D——, who was always ready to investigate a possible source of danger.

We went outside into the darkness and listened. One or two shots rang out from time to time, but we could tell from the sound that some of them were from our side, so that evidently the snipers were being answered back in their own coin.

CHAPTER 9

Reinforcements

From now on my work became double, for I was the only A.D.C. left. Very early in the morning of the 25th October I accompanied the general on a visit to the various Brigade Headquarters. The mornings were very misty these days, and as a rule the heavy German shelling used to begin at 8 a.m. sharp. This was a Sunday morning, and what a lot we had gone through since the previous Sunday, when the great Battle of Ypres had started!

We first rode out to Kruiseik, to Brigadier-General R—— B——'s (20th Brigade) Headquarters.

We had to pass through Gheluvelt village, which was fearfully knocked about, and of course deserted some days since by its inhabitants. There were some dead men of ours lying on the side of the road, and dead horses. As we got nearer the Brigade Headquarters, which were approached by a by-road, we fell in with strings of wounded men, making their way, or being carried, back to the dressing station, which had been established in a farm on the right of the road, and luckily missed by shells. The mud at Kruiseik was awful. The whole place was ploughed up with craters of shells, a picture of desolation and havoc.

Dead horses were lying about everywhere, in those grotesque unnatural postures that horses killed in battle assume. We found Headquarters in that mood that is so splendid, yet so difficult to describe. "Thoroughly English" perhaps fits it best. It was the morning after that terrific night attack on our trenches in which the Scots Guards had lost so heavily. The staff in that little building conversed almost in whispers, out of consideration for the weary, sleeping officers who lay about on straw in the dark corners of the room.

I heard that poor Hugh Fraser had been killed. The Germans had come on in overwhelming numbers, and had succeeded in penetrating our line in half-a-dozen places. Having done so they had sat or stood about in the darkness, not knowing what to do next. Over and over again this same thing was noticed with regard to their attacks. Seemingly their orders only went so far as to tell them to carry the trenches. When they had done that they became like a lot of helpless sheep, and our reinforcements or counterattack, coming up, would slaughter them. So, it had been on this occasion. Our men had accounted for all the hosts of Germans that had swarmed in the darkness through the gaps which they had forced in our line.

And now the brigadier-general was giving my general the details. I stood near one of the two windows of the little building. They had both been darkened with boards, but whereas one had been made bullet-proof the other had not, and someone warned me just in time that I was standing by the wrong one. I moved slightly to one side, and a bullet "zipped" through and buried itself in the opposite wall. Although a slight swell in the ground outside hid the building from the Germans, and indeed from our own trenches, evidently some of their remarkably efficient snipers had taken up their position within view.

The noise woke up one of the sleepers. It was George P——. He gave me an account of that night. The Germans, he said, had broken through their line of trenches in several places, and had then hung about in clumps, seeming to have lost all initiative. He himself had found two of them sitting forlornly on a traverse of his trench! One large party had indeed occupied a building in rear of the line, and from there had opened a murderous reverse fire on the Scots Guards. It was then that Hugh Fraser met his death. He took a party of his men to surround the house. They bayoneted the Germans, but he himself was shot dead. Poor Fraser, he was a great loss. At Lyndhurst, just before we started, I had met his mother, Alice Lady Lovat. A couple of nights before his death, Hugh had come to our Headquarters with a dispatch. He was dog-tired, had been resting on a settee in the dining-room and had left it for an instant. He, poor fellow, got on to it immediately, and was fast asleep when I returned.

George P—— told me that the Germans had come on singing hymns and cheering. They had called out to our men in English, bidding them not to fire, as they were the Border Regiment. Words of command, too, had been shouted by them at our men, such as "'B' Company, Scots Guards, not to fire, as 'A' Company is going to cross their front!" "Captain P—— wanted out here, sharp!" etc., etc. Many officers were called upon by name. Some, it is said, went out: never, of course, to return.

I mentioned this occurrence in one of my letters home, and my mother sent the account to *The Times*. "How do they know?" it was headed. Curiously enough I saw it in the paper when I was in Guy's Hospital. Sometime afterwards I read in *The Times* the reply to my question, as it had appeared in a Cologne newspaper. The writer was very sarcastic, saying that German officers had taken the trouble to learn foreign languages, that therefore they could interrogate prisoners, and that "even poor barbarians" could study a foreign Army List. That was all very well, but a Scots Guards officer in London afterwards told me that his regiment had been opposed on the night of that attack to a Saxon corps whose officers they had but lately entertained in London!

P—— told me among other things that the Border Regiment on their right had hung on to their section of trenches in a most heroic manner. He said that they were "ever and always to be depended upon."

After a while my general and General R—— B—— left the little building in which we were and went into a "dug-out" in front of it. I waited with the horses and took the opportunity of giving boxes of the best Turkish cigarettes to all the officers I saw. These cigarettes had been sent out by some kind friend to our Headquarters Staff (by Colonel B—— I think). But we had thought it only right that we should pass them on to the fellows who had been through so much more than we had.

I met F—— of the Queen's, looking very pale and done-up. He was an old friend of mine, and we had been in Lady Roberts' Home in Murree together in 1907 when we were convalescent after enteric. He told me what his experiences in the trenches during these last few awful days had been. He said that the ghastly wounds on all sides were the hardest sights to bear.

For some reason the usual shelling did not begin that morning at the accustomed hour, and we rode back to our *château* unmolested. The general remained at his post at Headquarters until the afternoon. Many a time had he deplored to me the modern practice of tying the general to the end of a telephone wire. But the complaint of his staff was that he was far too little at the end of the wire, or rather at the centre of all wires, but miles away in front, practically in the firing line.

It was a delicate matter, of course, for the staff to show their disapproval, and only D——, who possessed the courage of his convictions in a singular degree, ever dared (at least to my knowledge) to do so. For one thing there was always the chance—nay, certainty—of some very winged words by way of rejoinder.

"I know what's wrong with my staff," I once heard the G.O.C. say irritably, "I've not had enough of them hit yet!"

But he did not in the least bit mean it, and always after these little ebullitions of feeling—due to the awful strain of the situation and to the almost constant pain which he suffered from the loss of his eye some years before—he would make an off-hand, but generous and charming, *amende.*

By about 2.30 p.m. that day (25th October) the general's impatience for what he called "the real thing" had become beyond control. The reinforcing movement of the First Army (1st and 2nd Divisions) had carried the whole of our line forward, though keeping Kruiseik as a pivot, which meant that our 21st Brigade, which had had its Headquarters at Veldhoek, had pushed these forward. (The 22nd were now, as has been seen, in reserve behind Veldhoek while, of course, the 20th were at Kruiseik.) The 21st Headquarters had, in fact, pushed forward to a little *château* near Pozelhoek, and thither the general announced his intention of going.

I shouted for the horses, which were always ready at hand. The general asked D—— to accompany him and, of course, I went too. We took a groom and a spare horse each. Tom, therefore, came with me. I rode "Dawn" and he "Brightness."

The enemy was very close to our positions at this time and his shells were searching the ground over which we had to ride. However, we got to the *château* all right, crossing some ploughed fields and jumping some of our discarded trenches on the way. The little *château* stood in well-wooded pleasure-grounds, and must have been a beautiful place in peace time. But the shrapnel cracking and swishing in the trees overhead, and the "Black Marias" coughing great craters in the ground, made everything of a peaceful garden nature lose its savour.

We rode along a ride between high laurel-planted banks, and at last got to the house. We sent the horses with the grooms to get what shelter they might in a deep part of the wood. (My general once said to me what a pity it was that nobody had ever invented a collapsible horse, which one could hang on a rack when not in use and take down again when required.) There was a sort of a tower or turret in the *château*, and up this I climbed to see what there was to be seen. The crazy

GERMAN AND ALLIED OPERATIONS, ARTOIS AND FLANDERS,
SEPTEMBER–NOVEMBER, 1914

staircase swayed under me as I climbed. Some of the steps were missing, where bits of shell had torn their way through. I peeped into a few of the rooms on my way up, and a pitiable sight they presented! Through holes in the floors and ceilings beds and other pieces of furniture had half fallen. Articles of clothing were littered about everywhere.

I remember particularly noticing a large straw gardening-hat, such as is worn by ladies, which was still hanging on a peg behind a shattered door. Our plucky young signalling officer had been using the tower as an observation-station for a long while, and the Germans had been doing their utmost to destroy it. While I was up there four shells came in a covey and pitched just short of it in the garden outside. I saw four craters, spaced most accurately, and looking like inverted flower-beds, form in the middle of a grass plot down below me. I clambered hastily down and the three of us ran forward to some out-buildings where we found Brigadier-General W—— with his staff, and the officers of the Scots Fusiliers, which regiment was holding that portion of the line.

We remained for a time talking to the brigadier. German snipers' bullets were flattening themselves against the walls of the out-houses behind which we were sheltering and whenever we looked out in the direction of the enemy we were promptly fired at. Our red caps made a conspicuous mark for sharpshooters, and General W—— begged my general not to show himself, or at least to remove his cap. He took it off for about half a minute and held it behind his back, but very soon he forgot all about it and put it on again. After a bit we said goodbye to the Scots fusiliers' officers (a very cheery lot) and went off to a gate that looked west at the other end of the *château* grounds, to witness the advance of one of our regiments, the Yorkshires.

It was a stirring sight to see the thin lines going steadily on. But we knew them to be too thin, for alas! there were not enough men available to put any weight into the thrust. One realised that the forward movement must soon cease. While we were there a bullet smacked against the brick-work pillar of the gate quite close to my general, but the shells, fortunately, went on plunging into a certain plot of ground in the garden, well clear of us and the others. We retraced our steps to the *château* and from there I was able to spot an enemy's observation post on the tower of the little church at Pozelhoek. I took the bearing of it with my prismatic compass, and we sent a message to our divisional artillery to do the needful.

While we were there, the *château* was struck two reeling blows by "Black Marias," but no splinters came very near us. Immediately to the north of us we could see one of the reinforcing regiments advancing to the attack. They seemed to be in fairly full strength, and it was an exhilarating thing to see a battalion in such a condition—so different from ours.

While we were here, at about 4 o'clock in the afternoon, the general dictated to D—— and me an order to all three brigades, to say that the French and our First Army were advancing on our left. Our 2nd Division was taking for its general objective, Becelaere in the first instance, and Terhand in the second. The 4th Brigade of that division would keep in touch with our left. Our division was to advance its left, in the first instance, as might be necessary in order to keep touch with the 2nd Division, using Kruiseik as a pivot. Our 21st Brigade was to keep touch on its left with the 4th Brigade, and with the 20th Brigade on its right. Our 20th Brigade was, in the first instance, to maintain its position on the pivotal point of Kruiseik, and to be prepared to advance as required later. Our 22nd Brigade was to remain in divisional reserve.

It will be seen how important the right of our line had become (*i.e.* Kruiseik, and behind it Zandvoorde) from its being made the pivot upon which our advance (or our retreat) was to turn.

While we were still at the Pozelhoek *château* the advance of the grenadiers (4th Brigade) continued, though not very fast. A party of their officers joined us where we were standing behind the *château*, and among them was young G——, my general's brother in law. The general remarked to me how curious it was to see so typical a "young-man-about-town" amid our present surroundings.

After another visit to Brigadier-General W——, we decided to return to our own Headquarters, from which we had been a long time absent. We therefore went to where we had left our horses, and found that D——'s had been slightly wounded by a shell splinter. On the way back "Brightness" got rather caught up in some barbed wire, being very restive; but fortunately she was not cut.

About this time, we moved our Divisional Headquarters on about half a mile, to a *château* that stood just off the Ypres-Menin road, on the left, immediately opposite the one in which I had heard Mass on the 18th October. This new place of shelter, although still intact, was very much the worse for wear. It, too, had been left by its occupants "all standing," but the Germans who had made use of it had left it in a filthy condition. I had to get a fatigue party to clean it up a bit. It had possessed a good cellar, stocked with every kind of wine and liqueurs, but of these only the red wine and liqueurs were left, the Germans having drunk all the champagne, and hacked the doors of the white wine cellar open with their swords and bayonets.

The 26th October was about the most strenuous day I had, and with it commenced the period of chaos and desperation. The small move forward of our Headquarters had been undertaken more for the sake of going forward than from any other motive, and for the next couple of days it was to seem that our position was much too advanced for us to avoid destruction in the case of a bad setback.

I think we rode to 20th Brigade Headquarters twice that morning. On our way back through Gheluvelt the second time we met the Duke of Westminster driving his motorcar merrily along the road straight in the direction of the enemy. I had to gallop after him and warn him of his danger. He said he was only having a "look round." A little while later I met a battalion of the Scots Guards marching in column of route in the same direction going into action. I heard my name called by someone at their head. It was B——, whom I had known when he was A.D.C. to General Pulteney at Cork. The last time I had met him was during the season in London, on a Sunday afternoon at the Zoo. How different now! We shook hands, and I wished him luck. He was killed within an hour.

I also met D——, our A.A. and Q.M.G. here. He had ridden on to accompany his regiment a bit of the way into action. My General had galloped off in an unknown direction after saying something about going to our Headquarters, and when I got to the *château* nobody knew his whereabouts. I had a fine chase looking for him that morning.

I first got to the Headquarters of an Artillery Brigade, Colonel L——'s, but my general was not there. So, I decided to go to those of the 21st Brigade the *château* where we had stayed so long the day before. But as there was no immediate hurry, and my mare needed a rest, I loosened her girths and watered and fed her. There was a pile of carrots outside the little farmhouse where I was, and I added some of these to the feed, which had done a sort of paperchase along the road owing to a spent bullet having penetrated the nosebag. A kind gunner put a few stitches in it for me, and while the mare was feeding, I went forward to the shelter of a haystack, and watched some of our batteries at work. Away to the right front the enemy's artillery was once more making a target of poor Gheluvelt, through which we had just come. The Scots Guards must have been in the middle of it by now. I saw the church steeple, which had hitherto escaped, struck by a shell, and crumble into dust. The whole village was enveloped in flame and smoke.

The battery-sergeant-major told me that he had seen the general riding in the direction of the wood straight ahead of us, in which was the *château* that I had intended to visit. I mounted and rode off in its direction. I passed a battalion of the Queen's Regiment entrenched on the side of the road, awaiting their turn to move forward. I had to bide my time until a burst of shelling from the enemy had subsided. Every now and then there would be a long whistle and humming noise, and a shell would go cracking into the ground, sending up a dense cloud of black smoke mixed with earth. Some fell short of me, and others went over. One was within a few yards of where I sheltered. Another fell on the road by which I had just come, and I knew there had been casualties from the way the doctors and stretcher-bearers moved immediately to the spot.

Choosing what I hoped might be a lucky moment, I galloped across country to the *château*. My mare took some trenches in her stride, but at one point, in the open, she stumbled, and was almost on her head. When I got to the *château* the general was not there. I found young G—— still in the same spot, with some of his brother officers. It was very hot while I was there, the enemy having got the range of the building most exactly. O——, our signalling officer, came up after a bit, and I heard from him that my general had just got back to Headquarters from another portion of the line. We set off together, therefore, riding across country to our new *château*. When I saw my general, he did not ask me where I had been, and had probably forgotten having sent me off in pursuit of "Bend Or's" motorcar.

When seeing to the stabling of the staff horses, I noticed a funny old motorcar that had been turned out of its garage to make room for our horses. It must have been one of the earliest motors ever made. It was exactly what is suggested by the now-forgotten term "horseless carriage," and a most antiquated type of carriage at that.

CHAPTER 10

An Anxious Time

In the afternoon occurred about the most dreadful thing I saw in all my experience of the Front. A biplane, which I certainly took to be one of ours, was circling about over our heads, at a very low height, dropping coloured lights. I realised that she was signalling by means of these to our batteries; but apparently no warning or announcement had been made to the men of a new division with which the main road was literally crammed at that time. The 'plane continued to circle over our heads, and everything seemed to be going right. Suddenly one of our staff officers came galloping in to Headquarters, and as he dismounted, I heard him say, "I am positive it's an enemy. The instant it dropped those lights about half-a-dozen 'Jack Johnsons' came and blew a lot of our fellows to pieces immediately under it. I don't care if it has a Union Jack painted on it," he continued, in reply to a remark made by someone, "if it has it's a spy, that's all!"

While he was yet speaking a dreadful thing happened. The massed thousands of troops opened fire with their rifles on the helpless target. Never before had I heard an absolutely continuous roar of musketry. One knows what a well-executed *feu de joie* is like. This was like a thousand of them, so fired that there was not the minutest interval between the shots. One's agonised gaze was glued to the aeroplane. Gunner officers came running from the concealed batteries and from inside the *château*, shouting that it was our own machine. I heard one of them having a heated, despairing argument with the staff officer who had brought in the report. It was like watching the butchery of some noble animal, but rendered infinitely worse by the knowledge that there were two human beings in the machine—two of our own officers.

With such a stream of bullets coming at it, it was impossible that the aeroplane could escape being hit over and over again; but one hoped against hope that it might have time either to climb or to descend to safety. Suddenly it wobbled and began to swoop. Then a bright flame burst from it. A cheer went up from the massed troops—a cheer and a laugh. Never did cheering or laughter sound more cruel. They, of course, thought that they had done a meritorious deed. As the blazing aeroplane fell to earth one of the occupants was seen to fall out. He was dead, of course, when picked up; and his companion, who was still strapped in his seat, was burnt to a cinder. The machine, where it fell beyond the trees, was absolutely riddled with bullets. We afterwards learned the names of the poor lads.

Hearing the cheering and the horrified exclamations of his staff, my general came hurrying out of the *château*, where he had been at work in an inner room. He was immediately made aware of what had happened, and of course his indignation was very great. "Find out who started the firing!" he said to me. I got on "Dawn" and galloped off through the *château* grounds into the roadway, which was still blocked with troops. One and all denied that they had fired, and said that the firing had all come from troops farther east along the road. This was afterwards reported to have been the case.

There was to be no sleep for me that night. The general was becoming anxious about the pivotal point of Kruiseik, and the state of the whole of that portion of our line that had up to now been held by our 20th Brigade, behind which the 22nd had been brought as a support, as we have seen. Our 20th Brigade had not held on to the pivot point, but had fallen back somewhat. Unfortunately, the units of the reinforcing division had not yet taken up their position when this brigade fell back, so that there was a large and dangerous gap from south of Kruiseik to the Ypres-Menin road; and in front of this gap were the entrenched Germans. Darkness was coming on, and there was no time to be lost.

It was dark when I was sent off in a motor to Brigadier-General L——'s (22nd Brigade) Headquarters. I had to tell him that every available man he had was to parade at 11 p.m. to dig a new line of trenches. This was whipping a dead horse with a vengeance, for the 22nd Brigade had suffered terribly, and in spite of their having been for a couple of days in divisional reserve they were utterly tired out.

At the appointed hour my general took G—— and me with him on foot. We got to the starting point, and there we waited until the troops and tools were ready. It was a long wait, and I remember that I sat down on the step of a little wayside shrine and nearly fell asleep.

The night, alas! was to begin with another accident to one of our own officers, a young subaltern of Engineers being shot dead by a stupid sentry for not answering a challenge which probably he never heard. This occurred quite close to where we were.

After a while the general took the two of us forward into Gheluvelt. There we found the Regimental Headquarters of a battalion of the Black Watch. We ascertained from them the line which they were going to take up, and then we branched off a little way along the road towards Kruiseik. Here the general told us that he had arranged to meet some companies of the Cameron Highlanders (also belonging to the relieving division) and for about two hours we waited in the darkness.

It was cold and eerie work waiting there. Save for the occasional firing of heavy guns the night was absolutely still. The sky was "thick inlaid" with stars, and below the constellation of the Great Bear the comet that I had first seen at Lyndhurst was still faintly visible. The general was very impatient that night, and much put out at the non-arrival to time of some officers whom he had been expecting. G—— and I sat down on some straw in a barn. While we were in there, I heard the sound of somebody running down the road. I listened, and the footsteps ceased. I told my companion, and we went out and stood in the middle of the road with our revolvers ready. After a time, an N.C.O. came back along the road from the direction in which we had come and said that a German prisoner had escaped. He brought a small search-party with him, and they carefully searched the ditches on either side of the road, but without result.

Then two men came down the road from the direction of the enemy. One was very drunk, and it turned out that he had been wounded, and was being helped to the rear by a pal, who apparently had filled him up with rum to keep him cheerful. The drunken man was talking in broadest Scots. My general must have mistaken this for German, for suddenly we saw him dart across the road out of the darkness, pointing his revolver straight at the reveller's head. "Hands up! Hands up!" he cried. But the Scot only replied with an expression which is equally current in both Scots and English (though not in the politest circles), and the incident was closed.

When the two companies of the relieving division (or perhaps there were three) arrived, my general told me to lead them to take up a new line, which was to extend from Kruiseik (inclusive) north-eastward to a point some hundreds of yards short of the junction of the Kruiseik-Becelaere and Ypres-Menin roads, at which point they would get touch with the right of the Black Watch, who were newly dug in. I was to lead the column to Kruiseik, and to start laying out the line from there, until by extending to the left it joined up with the Black Watch. I was then to report to him in Zandvoorde village at daybreak, where he would be, the exact position which they had taken up, and its extent.

Now, the drawback to this was that the right of the Black Watch was not only in the air, but none of us knew, except approximately, where it was. It would be far safer, it seemed to me, if we first went to the road junction, got touch with the Black Watch, felt for their right flank, and then carried the line on from there to Kruiseik, which was at least something tangible and not very hard to find, even in the dark. The question of touch to the south of Kruiseik (with the left of our 20th Brigade) was going to be settled separately, by the 20th Brigade (?) occupying the line from the Zandvoorde Ridge to Kruiseik, which they were to fill up from the Zandvoorde end. When, or how, this was to be done, or whether it was to be done at all that night, I don't know. With regard to the further continuation, to the north, of the new line (which was at best a very patched-up affair, done in the dark) the Queen's were already dug in from the road junction northwards.

But orders were orders and we set off, and were soon swallowed up in the night. After stumbling along for about three-quarters of an hour we got to the wretched little group of houses that was Kruiseik. I had been marching at the head of the column with the colonel, McE——, and the adjutant, B——, afterwards killed. We had sent on a small advanced-guard on nearing the village, and when this had reported all quiet, we moved up and then halted. The colonel and I, with some of the other officers, went into the trenches lately vacated by our 20th Brigade. A large farm was blazing furiously to our right front. I could see the reflected glare from it lighting up a copse which must have been behind the enemy's line.

We soon realised how dangerous a thing it would be to attempt to gain touch with the Black Watch from that flank on such a night. The darkness was intense, and the country over which we should have to pass (for the new line to be entrenched was considerably back from the road) was intersected with trenches. True, the men were very tired, and there was not too much time before daylight. The line had to be selected and dug. But who knows that they would not have got out in front of the Black Watch line and been fired on had they started feeling for their flank in this groping way?

After a brief consultation with some of his officers the colonel decided to go round the other way after all, and we retraced our steps. Progress was very slow, and I don't think there were two hours of darkness left when at length we got by the main road to the Black Watch line.

By moving in single file along behind the line of digging Black Watch we were able to get a fair start for the laying out of our own line in prolongation of it. I had to bear in mind what my general had told me about reporting to him the exact position of the new line of trenches, and the extent it occupied. The direction I got from the North Star and, of course, as one end of the line rested on the road junction, which was clearly marked on the map, all I had to do was to pace the distance occupied by the Black Watch, and then to estimate the space that the Camerons would take up.

Pacing was no easy matter on such ground, however, in the dark; but I was able to arrive at a fairly accurate result. The ground was full of deep trenches already, many lines of which we had to cross. Discarded equipment lay about everywhere, and every now and then one stumbled over a corpse. When we got to the end of the Black Watch line, we continued the direction until all our men were strung out on the ground they had to dig. Sentries were posted and commanding points occupied. It was uncanny work leading that thin line of ghostly Highlanders across the ravaged country within a few hundred yards of the enemy. I could hear the shouts that arose from their trenches, snatches of song, too, and the incongruous strains of many gramophones.

Having done all I had been told to do, I took leave of the colonel of the Camerons. He said that I might take his horse if I wished, for otherwise it would have been impossible for me to get to Zandvoorde in time to catch my general, as I had a long way to go. The horse would only be an encumbrance to him, he said, and I might send it back when I got an opportunity. I was only too pleased to take it. I found it in a building a little way back along the road. It was the poorest thing in chargers imaginable, and it was as much as I could do to get a slow trot out of it now and again. However, it got me back to the *château* at Veldhoek, passing safely one or two bad places within easy range of which German snipers generally lay up.

Passing through gaunt and ravaged Gheluvelt I came upon a house, seemingly intact, through the windows of which there came what looked like the friendly glow of lamplight. But all was deathly quiet inside it, and the glow proceeded, I discovered, from the smouldering rafters, which had been set on fire by a shell. Constantly this happened to me in passing through deserted villages by night, yet I always felt a sense of chill and horror, brought about by the difference between expectation of companionship and realisation of intensified loneliness. It used to remind me of an adventure which once befell me on some manoeuvres in India, when, having lost my way in front of the outposts in the dark, I saw a fire blazing in the distance, which turned out when I got to it to be the funeral pyre of some poor victim of the plague.

Day was just beginning to dawn as I got to the *château*. D——, the ever-wakeful, was up when I dismounted in front of the entrance. He told me that the general had not been there during the night. So, I merely waited long enough to change the tired old "skin" that I was riding for "Dawn," and out I set again for Zandvoorde.

On my way I passed some of our batteries, just beginning to prepare for the business of the day again, and looking uncomfortable and dishevelled. I also saw S——, and hailed him where he stood in a field some distance from the road. He, too, had been up all night, and he shouted something about having lost the general. I pushed on up a hill to the south of the little hamlet of Zandvoorde, and then rode along the top of the ridge into the place. Nowhere could I see any sign of the general, and the village was absolutely deserted. I could see no indications at all of any British troops on the ridge, and I supposed the dismounted cavalry must be well down the forward slope, hidden in the mist. A good deal of enemy firing was going on, and streams of machine-gun bullets were coming over the crest.

I rode quickly on into the village of Zandvoorde, with its quaint pyramidal church tower, all knocked about; and a little way down the hill on our side I came upon the C.R.E., standing by the general's motor. But there was no general! The C.R.E. told me that he had found him quite impossible to keep with. The motor had been ordered to wait in the spot where I found it until a certain hour, which was now past.

Now, whether I was right or wrong in doing what I afterwards did, I do not know. But it seemed to me that the Zandvoorde Ridge was in danger, and that it was "up to me" to warn what troops I could on my way back to Headquarters—troops, that is to say, that were in support in the immediate vicinity, and batteries of artillery. These only amounted to some two companies of the Queen's and two batteries, and these I put on the *qui vive*. After that I rode on to the "horseless-carriage" *château*, to find that my general had not returned there even now. His staff were in a state of great uneasiness at his non-appearance. Fortunately, the commander of the Fourth Corps was there, however, and to him I made my report.

My general arrived later in the morning, and took some much-needed rest in a darkened room of the *château*. One really was a "Galloper" in those days, in addition to an A.D.C. A good share of the general staff work in the field fell to one's lot, though, of course, one had even less right than the real Staff Officer to order anything on one's own initiative. But it seemed to me on this occasion imperative to warn the units I did of the danger which appeared to threaten the Zandvoorde ridge.

Being pretty tired myself, as may be imagined, I went into an upstairs room of the *château* and threw myself on the bed there. In spite of the terrific din I slept soundly for three hours. It was about an even chance that a shell would strike the *château*, for just outside in the garden was one of our batteries, cunningly concealed by branches, which the enemy's guns and aeroplanes were trying hard to locate. All his shells, however, seemed to be falling short, and the *château* was not hit.

That night (27th-28th October) a divisional order was issued stating that we were attached from today to the First Corps. The 2nd Division, on our left, were stated to have made good progress; the French had done likewise; and the Belgians had successfully held their own. The enemy had had to call for assistance.

We were to occupy a defensive line with one brigade, the other two being held in reserve. Energetic reconnaissance and patrol work were to be carried out by day and night.

It was just as well that the general was able to snatch those few hours' sleep that day, and to me they were of inestimable value, too, for I had to be up at three the next morning to accompany him on a reconnaissance which was to start at 3.30. The only entry in my notebook for that day (the 28th October) is "Fighting, fighting, fighting," Somewhat laconic; but one had little time, or even inclination, for the keeping of a diary, and what time I did get I usually devoted to scribbling letters home.

But I remember that at the appointed hour the general, Colonel M——, and I set off. It was pitch dark as we rode out of the *château* grounds. I was riding "Dawn" again, poor "Brightness" having been shot by a sniper the previous morning while I was having my short sleep.

Being anxious to get Colonel McE——'s charger (which he had lent me) back to him, I had told Tom to ride "Brightness" out, and to lead the colonel's horse. He had started out with another groom for company, but riding the colonel's horse, I think, and all had gone well until he reached a certain point on the road beyond Gheluvelt. There a bullet had caught the poor little chestnut in the back, right through the kidneys. She had "sat down," Tom told me, and died very soon. He and the other man had had to take refuge from a burst of shell-fire in a house by the side of the road, until it was possible for them to return. Poor "Brightness"!

Tom had a narrow escape. Fine lad, best type of Irishman, would he had always been as fortunate!

The general met some other officers by appointment at a little cottage where the 21st Brigade Headquarters had been established. As we now belonged to the First Army, we came under the orders of Sir Douglas Haig, Sir E. Rawlinson having gone home to superintend the completion of the 8th Division, which should have formed the other half of his corps (the 4th). I was left for about an hour at the farm in charge of the horses, and when the general rejoined me after a reconnaissance on foot we rode to Klein Zillebeke, where we found Brigadier-General L——, and the Headquarters of the 22nd Brigade. We rode back to Veldhoek through the woods, and very beautiful the larches looked in the early morning autumnal light.

CHAPTER 11

Going "All Out"

Shortly after we had got back to the *château* the shelling became very severe. Several men and horses were hit in the pleasure-grounds. Some gun teams that were being exercised in a ring on an open plot in front of the hall door had a narrow escape, for a shell burst in the middle of the plot without hitting anybody. The men seemed perfectly unmoved, and continued quietly to circle round, until they were ordered to desist. A second shell burst among a group of horses that were feeding, and when the smoke of the explosion had cleared away, I saw loose horses galloping about, and some lying on the ground. A man who had been badly hit was brought for treatment to the *château*, and as he lay there, he lit the inevitable cigarette, and tried to appear unconcerned.

Things were getting too hot for Headquarters, and the general gave the order to return to our former *château* near Hooge. We rode over there together, and once more established ourselves in the old familiar quarters. I had one or two messages to carry during the day, but no salient fact remains in my memory concerning them. Vincent, the cook, provided the needed element of comic relief. He could hardly be induced to leave the Veldhoek Château, where, in the capacious underground kitchens, and with the well-stocked cellar, he had thoroughly enjoyed himself. I had had to post a sentry with fixed bayonet over the cellar, to prevent the numerous soldier-servants, cooks, etc., from helping themselves to wine; but Vincent, by virtue of the complete control which he had acquired over everybody below stairs, was privileged.

The result was that when I gave the order for the whole establishment to get on the move, the cook was far too happy to want to go. He was talking a sort of *lingua franca* which he had picked up, I suppose, during many years of voyaging at sea. (He had long been a ship's steward.) He was absolutely the last man to leave the ship, and when he went, he carried with him a dozen of Burgundy for our mess, rightly urging that there could be no point in leaving it behind.

Before we left Veldhoek Château (in the afternoon of 28th October) a divisional order was issued to say that the 1st and 2nd Divisions were continuing their attack, and that we were to be prepared to co-operate. For the time being we were to remain on the defensive line from where the left flank of the cavalry was entrenched (a *château* about half a mile to the east of Zandvoorde) to the Ypres-Menin road at the ninth kilometre stone.

This line was divided into two sections, and each of the brigades in turn was to hold a section, passing from left to right, the odd brigade going into reserve. As few troops were to be used in the trenches as was consistent with safety. Trenches were to be improved as far as possible, and a second line provided for the use of the garrison during the day. When in reserve, 20th and 21st Brigade were to concentrate at Hooge, and 22nd Brigade just east of Klein Zillebeke.

For the moment it seemed as if we were to have a breather. But next day, 29th October, was to be one of very severe fighting. A "counterattack" was ordered to be carried out by our division, against an enemy who had made very material progress in his attack on the divisions that had relieved us. We had not the weight necessary to press such a counter-attack, home. It was carried out, none the less, with great gallantry and determination. After a preliminary success it was driven back by sheer weight of numbers.

In the very early morning, almost before it was light, I was on a mission which took me past the spot where poor "Brightness" had been shot. I saw a huddled heap lying on the side of the road, and I dismounted and struck a match to see if it was she, hiding the flame as well as I could from the direction of the snipers.

"Brightness" was a chestnut with no marks whatever save a faint star. I was able to recognise her by this, as well as from the hole that the bullet had made right through her back, just behind where the saddle should have been. The saddle had been looted, of course, and the bridle, but I salvaged the head-collar, which was still on her.

In the afternoon the general wished to witness the progress of our counter-attack from close quarters, and he took N—— and me with him. We had a Belgian motorcyclist attached to our Headquarters, and him the general ordered to accompany us as well. We rode off, with the cyclist puffing along behind us, until just beyond Gheluvelt the general suddenly wheeled his horse, put him straight at a big ditch,

First Battle of Ypres
Approximate positions, nightfall 29 October 1914

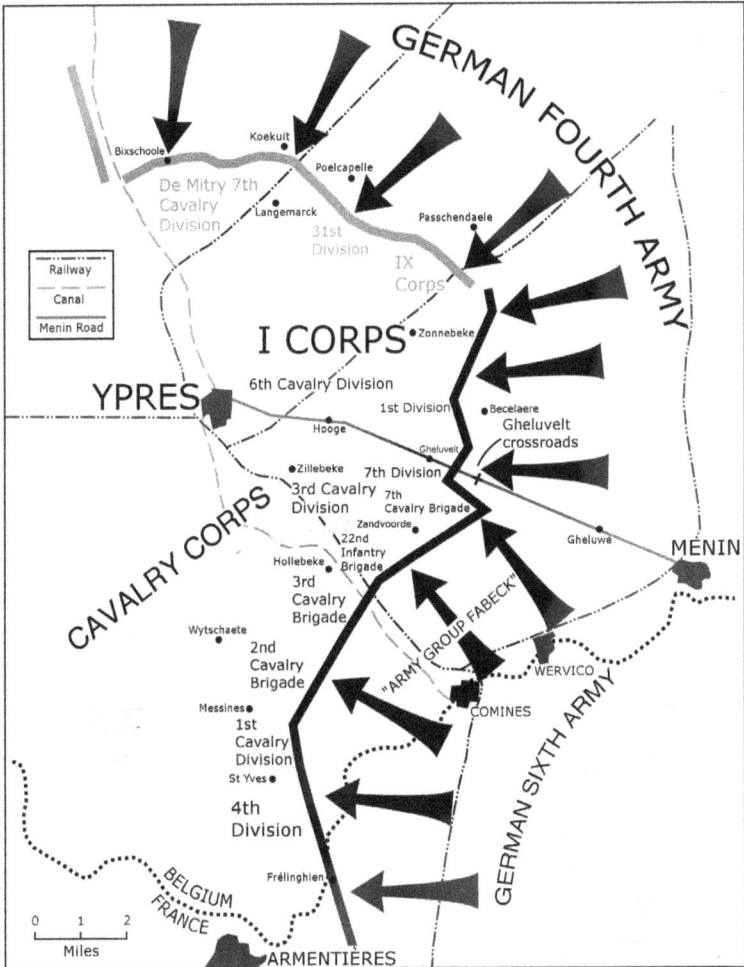

Bixschoole

Koekuit

Poelcapelle

De Mitry 7th Cavalry Division

Langemarck

31st Division

Passchendaele

IX Corps

GERMAN FOURTH ARMY

Railway

Canal

Menin Road

I CORPS

Zonnebeke

6th Cavalry Division

YPRES

1st Division

Becelaere

Gheluvelt crossroads

Hooge

Gheluvelt

Zillebeke

7th Division

3rd Cavalry Division

7th Cavalry Brigade

Zandvoorde

22nd Infantry Brigade

Gheluwe

MENIN

CAVALRY CORPS

Hollebeke

3rd Cavalry Brigade

Wytschaete

2nd Cavalry Brigade

"ARMY GROUP FABECK"

WERVICO

Messines

1st Cavalry Division

COMINES

St Yves

4th Division

GERMAN SIXTH ARMY

Frélinghien

BELGIUM

FRANCE

0   1   2

Miles

ARMENTIÈRES

and started to canter off across country towards Kruiseik. N—— and I followed him without difficulty, but the poor cyclist was naturally nonplussed, and must have been somewhat dismayed at the turn which things had taken, especially as he had been instructed not to let us out of his sight! We saw no more of him that day.

After witnessing part of the counter-attack and remaining for about two hours in some farm buildings where swarms of bullets from rifle and machine-gun fire went over us, we rode on to where we could interview General Byng and the Cavalry Staff. The cavalry were well in front of the Zandvoorde ridge now; but I don't know what sort of support was behind them. I think it was on the next day, the 30th, that the ridge was taken by the enemy.

We were on our way back to Headquarters when the general dismounted and said he must go back to see for himself what the new line our forces had taken up was like, and whether there were any gaps. We handed our horses over to the grooms, who were instructed to await our return, and we then followed the general back to the trenches. It was now dark, and it had started to rain hard. We walked across country through mud that almost drew the boots off one's feet. The general went along the whole of that long, straggling line, noting down in his notebook the composition of the forces that held it.

As we were going along one road—I think it led to Kruiseik—we heard pitiful groans proceeding from the ditch on one side of it. A poor wounded soldier lay there, dying. It was pitch dark now, and there were no ambulances or stretcher-bearers anywhere about. My general told me to stand by the poor fellow until he could send help from the trenches. I got down beside him in the cold, wet ditch. It was terrible to hear his groans, and quite impossible to think of anything to say to comfort him. He knew me for an officer, and it was pathetic to hear him say "Sir" to me—remembering to be polite even when his life was leaving him. I asked him where he was wounded, and something told me, even before he did, that it was in the stomach. He belonged to the Yorkshire Regiment.

All the while I sat there the cruel shells continued to scream overhead, and every now and again they hurled themselves into the wet clay, near where we were, as if still vindictively searching for the poor lad who was dying.

After what seemed an age an N.C.O. and three men appeared. They had no stretcher, but talked of taking the boy away on their rifles. But when I told them where he was hit, they said it would be better not to move him. I had to rejoin my general then. A young officer whom I stumbled across in the trenches said he would give the poor wounded fellow a morphia injection, which seemed the best thing to do.

I caught my general up, and for the next two hours he and N——and I trudged along through mud and slush trying to locate other trenches, and to complete our survey of the line. I was several times able to put him in the right direction, for my ears would catch the noise of pick and shovel, whereby we were guided. Many times, the general would have taken a wrong direction but for me, and it was plain to see that the prolonged strain was telling on his nerves.

After a very fatiguing time we fell in with some men who were going back to Brigade Headquarters for rations. We followed them until we got to the little building that sheltered the Headquarters. I think it was the 20th Brigade, but am not sure that the 21st were not there, too. A wounded officer of the South Staffords was sitting on one chair, with one leg propped upon another. He had been hit in the shin. I stayed in the outer room while my general conferred with the brigade commanders in an inner one, and after a long time we set out for the spot where we had left the horses. On our way there we met many horsed-ambulances lumbering along the unmetalled road, coming to fetch their freight of wounded. One could dimly hear the same rumbling going on on the other side of the ridge where the Germans were, quite close. It really seemed as though there was a mutual tacit agreement not to fire on these painful vehicles of mercy.

We got to the horses after a long walk. What a cold and weary vigil they had had, waiting for us all those hours! Luckily the general's motor was there, too, and he went on in it; while N—— and I and the grooms trotted the horses home to Hooge.

Even that night I had the greatest difficulty in getting the general to eat anything, but when the other officers had given up expecting him, and the fragrant stew of bully beef which my cook had prepared had got cold, he came in to my great relief and asked for some of it. I produced, too, some of the excellent Burgundy that Vincent had brought with him when we left the other *château*. The general, who had deprecated our drinking any wine or spirits during the campaign, was very glad of this Burgundy. It amused me, though, when after drinking good part of a bottle he suddenly said to me, "I hope this isn't looted!"

The 30th October was another critical day, but for me it was something of a rest, as I was left behind in the Château Beukenhorst to deal with urgent messages, and to direct staff officers, etc., to our new headquarters. These were established for the day at a farm one mile east of Zillebeke.

Except for Major B——, our veterinary officer, and a few signal operators, I was left all alone for most of that day in the *château*. My groom remained with my two horses in the stables, and all three got some much-needed rest. B—— and I made a small fire in the little study, for it was a cold, wet day. From time to time staff officers and messengers would arrive, whom I would direct on to the new Head-quarters, and in particular one officer of high rank came and pointed out on my map a certain *point d'appui* on our right, which we were to hold on the morrow at all costs.

When the Divisional Headquarters rode off towards Zillebeke they left the whole of the Headquarters transport behind, to be dealt with by me. All that I could discover was that I was to send it to a place of safety, of course at no great distance. I accordingly dispatched the vehicles to various destinations, mostly into Ypres.

S——, our G.S.O. 2, whom I met during the afternoon, told me that he had spent the morning in making a personal reconnaissance of the situation on our right. At 11 o'clock the right of the 22nd Brigade had been thrown back across the Basseville stream, with the Gordons moving up behind the South Staffords to get into position to attack westwards in conjunction with them, Zandvoorde being the objective. Two battalions which were in Corps Reserve, under General Bulfin, were moving through the woods about Klein Zillebeke, and, if the opportunity arose, one of these battalions was to support the attack of the South Staffords and Gordons, while the other was to dig in in rear. A Field Artillery Brigade—the 35th, I think—was to support the attack.

As the afternoon wore on it became evident that at all events the enemy was not making any very great headway, at least in our part of the field. Towards evening our Headquarters were re-established in the Château Beukenhorst, and word was sent to D—— to bring up the supply column from Ypres. At 5 p.m. a message came from 1st Army Headquarters to say that the 1st Division's Headquarters were "between fifth kilometre stone and V of Veldhoek," in other words, almost contiguous with our own. It will be remembered that we now formed part of the First Army.

That night we issued an important divisional order for the morrow, 31st October, a date which was to prove, perhaps, the culminating point of the great German onslaught. The gist of it was that our division was to assist an attack which the right wing of the British (1st and 2nd Divisions), combined with French infantry, were to make early in the morning on the German positions between Hollebeke and Zandvoorde. Our co-operation was mainly to take the form of holding on to our present position, and to portions of the line vacated by the attacking troops, and of resisting counter-attacks.

Our divisional artillery was to support the attack. The essential necessity of holding on was impressed on all, and also of maintaining touch throughout. It was again pointed out that the construction of supporting trenches would obviate the necessity to keep all the troops in the firing line by day. All wheeled transport not actually required for righting was to be sent back to join the train, and the Ypres-Menin road was to be kept clear of vehicles. Divisional Headquarters were once more to be established at the farm one mile east of Zillebeke.

CHAPTER 12

The Breakthrough

October 31st. This most critical day was crammed full with incident. I can only set down some of the things in which I was involved myself, and in fact from this day onwards it would be absurd for anybody occupying the very subordinate position which I did to attempt to describe the events in a general sense.

The day started with a piece of news for me. Very early in the morning I heard that the 2nd Battalion of my regiment had sent an urgent application for me to join them. (This was the battalion that I had seen off from Rosslare in the beginning of the war, and with which I had unsuccessfully applied to go. They had suffered heavily in the retreat from Mons, and were now out of the line and being made up to strength again.)

One's duty is primarily with one's regiment, but when a second message arrived to say that they were at St. Omer, acting as "G.H.Q. Reserve" I really did not see why I should give up my Galloper's billet just yet. It was with many misgivings, therefore, that I rode out to our temporary Headquarters that morning, and I determined to ask my general for advice as to what I should do at the first opportunity.

Arrived at the spot, we put our horses away in a barn as usual, and stood about in small groups, or paced up and down a field that adjoined the farmhouse. Time spent in this way was trying; there was cover from view and nothing else, and even the cover from view was to a large extent nullified by the numerous Taubes that kept passing overhead, spying out the land. There was a dense belt of wood between us and the firing line, and over this the shells came screaming, bursting to the right and left, short and beyond. The enemy's guns systematically searched up and down and across, and every now and then they would concentrate a crushing fire on some particular spot,

100

generally where there were neither troops nor animals, punching craters in the fields, setting barns and ricks instantaneously alight, and sending up dense clouds of evil, acrid smoke.

Animals that had been left behind when the people of the farm departed so hurriedly were still grazing all over the place, until every now and then a shell would come and send them scampering off to some fresh spot. Pigs and chickens were enjoying a most unwonted degree of freedom, and not being confined within any limits were able to fend for themselves for food. The unfortunate watch-dogs were the most to be pitied, for in a great number of cases they had been left to starve on the chain. Our men often tried to release them, but in many cases, they had become so fierce that nobody dared approach them. I remember witnessing an amusing encounter between two diminutive pullets which, quite oblivious of the battle that was taking place all around them, were engrossed in a fight on their own account, gazing into each other's eyes in that intent way they have when fighting. Perhaps each blamed the other for the noise that was going on.

Another funny incident occurred when a shell landed full in the middle of a small circle of piglets. It scattered them in all directions, but not one of them was hurt. I could hear their concerted squeal high above the roar of battle. But we did not like pigs. They roamed at large everywhere, very hungry, and there were stories of their gnawing dead bodies, and even attacking the wounded.

My general was pacing up and down close to where I stood. He must have heard about my having been ordered to go to the 2nd Battalion of my regiment, and he asked me if I wanted to go. He was kind enough to add that he did not want to lose me. I replied that I hated the idea of leaving him, but that if my regiment wanted me, I was bound to go. He said that was the correct view to take of it. Then I pointed out, however, that they were to be right back at St. Omer, in G.H.Q. Reserve.

"That alters the matter," he said, "and I must see what I can do about keeping you."

While we talked a Taube flew over, on its way back to the German lines. It was at a good height. The general took a long look at it through the telescope which he always carried, and then called loudly for a rifle.

Young N—— was the first to get one, but he stopped to take aim at the aeroplane himself. This the general would not allow; but when the rifle was handed to him the aeroplane was out of range. Nevertheless, he took aim, and fired, but without result. I knew well how intensely he disliked the inaction to which even he had sometimes to submit, and this little incident seemed to put him into good spirits immediately.

After we had walked up and down again several times, from the farm to the edge of the wood, and back again, my general decided to send a message to General Bulfin. The line was being hard pressed, and though I knew my general had no intention of falling back, yet he knew that the strain of the last fortnight had told heavily on our men (what was left of them), and that it might come to their having to fall back in spite of him. So, I had to go and find General Bulfin's Brigade Headquarters and show him on the map exactly where we should endeavour to establish our next line of defence if we were forced to yield ground. I rode "Sportsman" that day, and he behaved very well.

Bulfin's Headquarters were not very easy to find. I knew there was a telephone cable along the ground, laid in the rides that in more peaceful days some landowner had cut in the pheasant-stocked woods. But when I got to some cross-rides I found that there were two cables, going in divergent directions, and unfortunately, I followed the wrong one for a time. The whole wood was being raked by shrapnel— "flailed" is the best word I can think of to describe it. The slender larches were being cut in two and scored in every direction. I got to the shelter of a high, concave bank, and pulled my horse into a walk. Just then some shells came very near me, plump into a farmhouse, and I saw on the side of the road a heap of 18-pounder cases, showing where one of our batteries had been. But it was there no longer, having wisely shifted its position. Yet the Germans, thinking they had located it permanently, still continued to shell the place.

The high bank afforded excellent cover, and as the shells were plastering the road, both ahead of and behind me, I decided to remain there for a bit, and to dismount and study my map. I had great difficulty in making my horse get closer in under the bank. He preferred to stick his rump out in the road, and nothing that I could do would make him get nearer. Every now and then would come a shrapnel burst, and a spatter of bullets, and it looked as though his obstinacy would get him caught. When a horse gets into such a mood it is no use striving with him, and I had to let him be.

I had only been under the bank for a couple of minutes when two men of the Gordons came wearily up along the road, taking advantage of any piece of cover they could find. They told me they had been back to get ammunition, and they enquired of me the shortest way to their battalion. This I was able to tell them, and there being now a slight cessation in the shelling, they started to move off, but I thought they looked very longingly at my bank. I could not send them into danger and remain behind myself, so mounting my horse I set out with the best show of unconcern I could assume.

Presently I came upon the supporting trenches of the Northamptons, very cunningly dug in (but still mere scrapes), and from an officer whose voice seemed to come from the bowels of the earth, I learned that I was right in front of General Bulfin's Headquarters, and that I should have to cast back considerably into the wood to reach them. I had a fairly open large space, or clearing, to cross, and I did so at a canter. Suddenly I found a biggish drain in my way. Unfortunately, "Sportsman" had an annoying way of jumping very big, and straight "up and down" at quite small obstacles. He did so now, with the result that my Staff cap flew off. Just then the shrapnel started coming over again, and I had to go back and pick up the cap, and leap the ditch twice more!

I found some French and British orderlies in the wood, holding officers' horses, and on reaching them I discovered that they were outside the Brigade Headquarters, which consisted of a large dug-out, or "funk-hole." In it were about seven officers, among them General Bulfin. It was dramatic meeting him in this way. Years before, in 1899, just prior to the outbreak of the South African War, my father had chosen him, then a young regimental officer, to accompany him to the Cape as his Military Secretary. This was General Bulfin's chance, and from that moment he had never looked back. Also, from that moment I had never set eyes on him till now.

When I had explained my mission, and shown him exactly our alternative position on the map, he said he hoped to heaven we were not contemplating any retirement. I said that we were not, but that this was a measure of precaution. He thanked me for my information, and I saluted and withdrew. I said a few cheery words to the French dragoon orderly, and rode back by a shorter way to Headquarters and my general.

Before long I had to go with another message to General Bulfin. This time I told him who I was, and his pleasure at hearing that I was the son of his old chief was very great. It was worth going through a lot for, was that moment.

When some days afterwards General Bulfin wrote to my mother

that on meeting me all his troubles had seemed to vanish he must have been drawing somewhat of a long and kindly bow, for shortly after my second visit to him I quite *suddenly* found his wood full of retreating men. I shall never forget the chill the sight gave me. It seemed that at last our resisting power had been shattered; at last numbers had prevailed; at last Nemesis had overtaken Britain for her sloth and unpreparedness; at last the apathy of so many of her sons had met with its deserts. But, oh! it did seem sad that *we* should have to suffer, and to admit defeat now, after our great stand!

On arriving back at our Divisional Headquarters at the farmstead I found there no general. His staff was there, but in a state of alarm and trepidation at his disappearance, and at the turn which affairs had suddenly taken. Men of the relieving divisions were pouring back on every side; even what was left of the mighty 7th was giving ground at last. Colonel M—— had to issue orders for the retirement of Headquarters; and certainly not an instant too soon, for we were within measurable distance of capture. I was ordered to pack up the mess into its motorcar, and to dispatch it with all speed to the Halte just east of Ypres. The staff rode off to that place, too, all except the missing general and young N——, who had been with him.

I could not go, of course, but I made up my mind to search about in the vicinity for my general, for whose safety I had begun to entertain grave fears. I rode back into the wood where I had last spoken to Bulfin, but officers of his brigade among the moving mass told me that he had long left his dug-out. The sight which met my eyes was enough to fill anyone with apprehension. Every ride and glade in the wood was filled with men, all coming back, back, back. It was only by getting into a cross-ride that I could withstand the torrent. They were not in a panic or moving out of a fast walk. Simply we could see that they were giving ground. And all the time the shrapnel flails were cracking overhead, men were falling forward on their faces, where the deadly leaded strings had caught them. I confess those were awful moments as I sat on "Sportsman" in the middle of that ride. There seemed nothing for me to do save to stay there. I had no orders, and for all I knew my general had been killed.

After what seemed an age somebody who was passing down another ride shouted to me that I had better be going as the Germans were quite close. I rode away at a canter to where our Headquarters had been at the farmstead, and after I had been there a little while to my great joy, I saw my general and young N—— coming towards me.

The general was quite cool and composed, but very angry that we had shifted our Headquarters back to Ypres in his absence. He asked me where the d—— I had sent the mess motor to, and why; but after a little while he grew quite cheery, as he generally did when the danger was really acute. The three of us mounted our horses and started to ride somewhat vaguely back with the retreating men—"fugitives" was perhaps too strong a term to use just now. Not shrapnel now, but "Jack Johnsons" began to fall in their groups of four all about the slight slope over which the human wave was retiring. We three trotted up to where a battery of field artillery was digging itself frantically in in the soft ground. I remember noting the despair almost with which those gallant gunners worked. It seemed so pitifully inadequate against shells, that scraping at the soil.

Then, just as we got abreast of the battery, there was a stupendous rattle and roar. The earth seemed to open at our feet. My horse reared and plunged violently, and then seemed to be trying to wrestle with that of the general. There was a deafening, horrible coughing *Wonk! Wonk! Wonk!!!* as three craters boiled up at our feet three craters, thank God, *not four.* Had there been a fourth shell I think it would have wiped out our little party and a couple at least of the guns. *There was no fourth*, almost an unprecedented occurrence, and I afterwards heard that the enemy's battery that had fired on us had only a moment before had one of its guns knocked to smithereens by a direct hit from one of ours.

"One doesn't know how well one can ride until this sort of thing happens," I said to my general.

"No," he replied, "the *haute école* isn't in it with us!"

We rode on until we struck the Ypres-Menin road, and then, turning right-handed, we got back to the entrance-gate of the Château Beukenhorst. We left our horses in some buildings on the side of the road and sat down just outside the gate. The road was covered with men, and a company was starting to dig in feverishly at right angles to it. There seemed to be a sort of pause in the retirement, but nobody appeared to know what was taking place, and the confusion was indescribable.

But from what we had already seen the breakthrough had not occurred on the front held by us, but on that on which the British attack was to have been made that morning. Several messages, too, which we received during the afternoon, showed that our battalions were "perfectly calm and ready to hold the ground" (to quote the words of one from 20th Brigade) if only the breakthrough on their right could be stopped. My general told me nothing about what he had seen and done during his long absence from Headquarters, but I could tell from his demeanour that he was proud of his division, and satisfied.

At about 4.30 p.m. my general wrote messages to each of his three brigadiers and told me to deliver them. At that moment N—— and I were the only two of his *entourage* within call.

In the midst of all the confusion, and while my general was engaged in hastily writing the messages, who should come along the shell-swept road from Ypres, ponderously and with much circumstance, but "The Gnome" and his armoured car. Young de Kherkhove was in it with him. They stopped opposite to us, in about the worst place they could have chosen. It was plain that they had no orders and did not know what to do, but the little "Gnome" was obviously anxious to be of use. My general happened to look up, however, and told them angrily to "take that damned thing away!" I couldn't help laughing at the ludicrous sight they presented as they slowly backed, turned and lumbered off.

CHAPTER 13

All Saints

How I was to find any or all of the three brigadiers in that inferno I did not know, but I rode up the Menin road towards Gheluvelt hoping for the best. As a matter of fact, I found two of them together, Generals L—— and R—— B——, within ten minutes. They were in a trench near the *château* that stood on the other side of the road from the "horseless-carriage" one. The messages were to tell them of a new line that was to be taken up, but I gathered from them that they had already selected a line from which retirement without grave danger would be impossible. They had but a handful of men apiece, and communication was badly interrupted.

I rode on again to look for General W——. I passed through the village of Veldhoek and turned right-handed along the Zandvoorde road. This ran along a slight ridge that was much exposed to the enemy's shell-fire. A few men of the Queen's were holding some trenches on either side of the road, and houses were burning fiercely on every hand. It was awful to hear the cries of wounded men in one of these. They called out "Sir, Sir," to me as I rode past. Fortunately, I saw that a very gallant major of the Queen's, whose name I don't recollect, but who was the same officer that I had met a few mornings before at Zandvoorde, was at hand with a few men to help them. "All right, sonny!" I heard him call out in reply to the agonised appeal of one poor sufferer, "I'll fix you up in half a jiffy!" A splendid officer he was, and I had often noticed him during those few strenuous days.

General W—— was nowhere to be found in the portion of the field where I had been told he might be, but an officer whom I met on my way back said that he had just located a battery of the enemy's heavy artillery, right out in the centre of the plain to the east of us. He was most anxious to convey the information to one of our artillery officers. I said I would do so, and went back with him to where we could obtain a view. There right enough, about 5,000 yards away, I could see what appeared to be a battery. I noted the position as well as I could on my map and went to find one of our Divisional Artillery Staff. On my way to Veldhoek I found a gunner officer, and told him of what I had seen. He went back with me along the road to see for himself, and when I pointed out the battery, he said he would send a message through to Artillery Headquarters about it. Late that night I showed my general himself the exact spot on my map, and I believe we succeeded in making things hot for that German battery.

On my way to another part of the field to look for General W—— I had again to pass through Veldhoek. I found General L—— there, but without any of his staff. He advised me to get back to my general, as the message had by this time become inoperative. We stood together for a time behind a house, and shells were crashing into the village all around us. Close to where we were, I could see a couple of doctors who had established a dressing-station under a hedge. There they were, pursuing their noble, ghastly work, quite unconcerned, and smoking cigarettes while the houses were falling almost on top of them.

I soon started off again for the gate of our *château*, "Sportsman" carrying me very well, but inclined to pull when the shells fell close behind us. One talks (before one has seen the reality) of horses that will stand fire or that won't; but really in a big show like this it is all a matter of their not knowing which way to run. And then after a day or two their first frightened bewilderment gives way to a sort of resigned, trustful apathy; which is just as well.

This 31st October was such a long and eventful day that it is not easy to remember the sequence of events, or to do anything more than relate what occurred to oneself. When I got back to the *château* gate, I found that the general had gone, but I must have met him shortly afterwards for I remember walking along the road with him and N—— when (it being now quite dark) a dismounted motorcyclist dispatch-rider, pushing his machine, almost knocked him down. The general was naturally annoyed, and he ran after the much-frightened man and gave him a good hard kick.

After a bit he sent me to the Halte outside Ypres to tell the members of his staff that they were to return to the Huize Beukenhorst.

"I only want my fighting staff, not the others," he said.

He meant that the administrative staff were to stay behind; but the next morning we had to get them *all* up, the division into widely separated parts having proved most inconvenient. While at the Halte I got a little food—bully beef and jam—and was able to give "Sportsman" a much-needed rest and feed. I was standing in the road talking to young de Kherkhove when I saw a Red Cross motor-ambulance coming towards us from the direction of the battle. It was crammed with wounded, and seated on the step of the driver's seat was a young woman in khaki whom I recognised. It was Lady Dorothie Feilding. When last, I had seen her, it was Ascot week, and she had sat next to me in the theatre, and been one of our party at supper at the Savoy. What a change! She looked pale and tired, and no wonder. She had been at this work almost since the beginning of the war.

I had another long ride that night, in the darkness, to find my general. I found some squadrons of the 10th Hussars, and a French Cavalry Regiment, forming up behind a wood for some enterprise that was afoot. A senior officer of one of our staffs fell in with me and told me that he was trying to collect French infantry to aid in it. I was able to help him in talking to the colonel of the French Regiment, his own French being scanty. After that I got news of my general, and finally ran him to earth in a house in Hooge village, where I found a conference going on between high British and French staff officers. It was now quite evident that the battle had been, somehow or other, restored. The Germans were not coming on. It is hard to realise, when one knows one's own side to be almost wiped out, that the pause that ensues is owing to the enemy being for the moment powerless too. After a long dreary wait until the conference was ended, I accompanied the general back to the Château Beukenhorst. We found it still almost unharmed. That forenoon it had seemed certain we should not see it again.

We all made our "beds" down that night on the floor of the dining-room, ready to be up and off at a moment's notice. As I lay there, too tired to sleep, I heard a message come in to the effect that our 2nd Battalion had definitely been made into General Headquarters troops at St. Omer. They had, therefore, been withdrawn from the fighting, in which they had suffered so terribly, to be reconstituted. Next morning, I told the general this and he said "Now you must not go."

The 1st November, All Saints' Day, we established our Headquarters again at the farm. The first day we had gone there we had found a poor old bedridden man, who had been abandoned by his family when they fled away. I shall never forget his face when we appeared. He was very infirm, and only his eyes showed terror. But we took him out and gave him a little food, and then sent him into Ypres by motor. Probably this ride in so incredible a vehicle remains—if he be still alive—among his most fearful memories. On this morning (!) a young man and woman, and a little boy, suddenly appeared back to look for "*le vieux*." We told them he had been sent to hospital in Ypres, or he would have died.

I was busy taking messages that morning, and about mid-day, while the shelling was very severe, we saw a battalion of the grenadiers coming along the road from Zillebeke, over a ridge, the same battalion that I had met in the *château* below Pozelhoek. They must have done much trekking to be appearing now from exactly the opposite direction. I remember they selected for their five minutes' halt the very portion of the road where the shells had just been falling thickest. We watched them with bated breath, but it was not until they had fallen in again and were starting to move on that some shrapnel burst over them. At least one poor fellow was left behind, and we could see the doctor bending over him. Soon the battalion had reached the spot where our Headquarters were. Word came that the wood in front of us was full of Germans, and the grenadiers prepared to take it at the bayonet's point. They advanced into it in splendid style, but only found a few snipers there. We heard that the Irish Guards had been blown out of their trenches by German field-guns that had opened fire at 250 yards.

Later in the afternoon a report came that General Bulfin had been wounded, and before long he passed us on foot, going slowly back to the dressing-station, with some other wounded men. General Lord Cavan then assumed command of the 3rd Brigade. I was ordered by my general to do *liaison* with him, and to take two intelligent men of the Northumberland Hussars with me to carry messages. I was to keep my general informed of the situation in the wood just in front of us.

I took my men and we started off. We went on foot, as things were very hot, and we got to Lord Cavan's Headquarters (which were in a trench close to where General Bulfin's had been the previous day—so well had things been restored) without mishap. I stayed there about two hours, and sent some reassuring messages back by my two orderlies.

It was nasty work in that wood, for we were constantly shelled by both the enemy's guns and by our own. The tops of the fir-trees came tumbling down all about the wood. There was a little cottage close to us where a dressing-station had been established, and a constant stream of wounded men came to it. There was a pump behind it, and many men came for water from the trenches, each one carrying about a dozen water-bottles. I remember noticing what a brilliant red the doctor's hands and arms were.

It was very muddy where I had to stand, and I collected a few German helmets, and stood on these. A dead Boche lay quite close to our trench, staring up at the sky, his great shaven head looking horribly repulsive.

A big shell landed plump into a pretty little house not far from the dressing-station, and in a trice the whole thing was in a blaze. It seemed impossible that a solid thing like a house could catch fire instantly in that way. My general came up after a time, saying he could not remain inactively at our Headquarters. He hissed at me "You've given me no food!"

This was a bit hard. I had had lunch all ready for him back there at the farm, in spite of all the work I had got through. He had not eaten any then, and of course a time had come when it had all to be packed up and sent with the motor out of harm's way. I had been doing responsible work as *liaison* to Cavan, and it really seemed to me that one of the others might have taken up my task of trying to tempt the general into eating something.

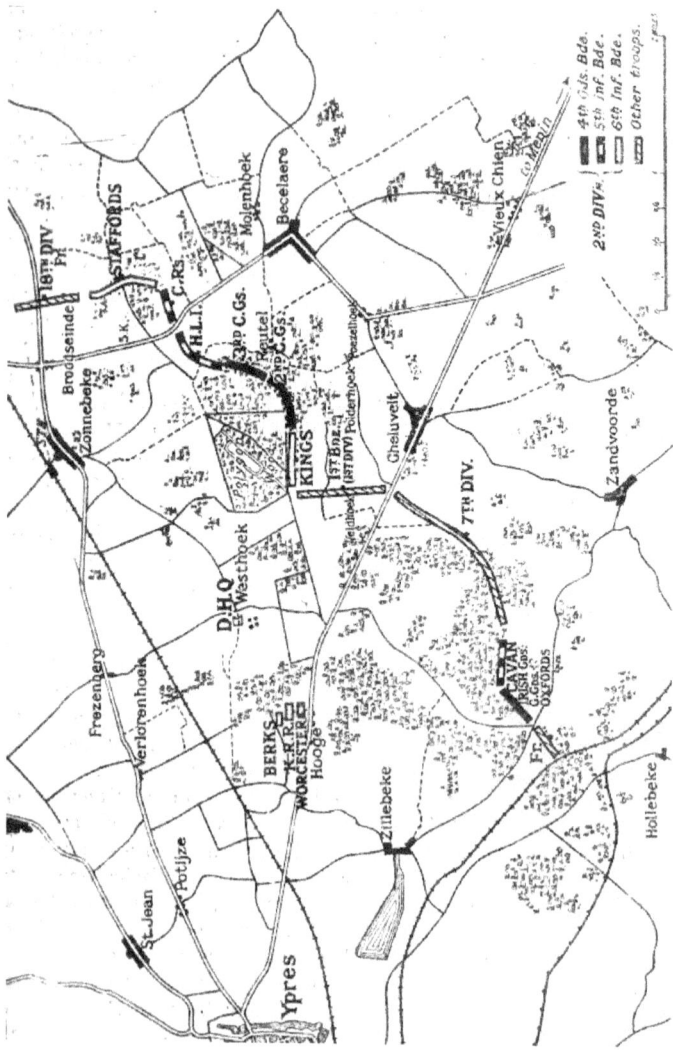

BATTLE OF GHELUVELT, 1ST NOVEMBER, 1914

CHAPTER 14

I Retire from the Contest

That night we spent again at the Château Beukenhorst. It passed safely, and at 4 o'clock I was up and ready for what the day might bring. It was 2nd November. Daylight saw Headquarters moved once more to the farm. I chose "Dawn" to ride that day, and told Tom to take "Sportsman." Just as we were moving off, however, we found that "Sportsman" was dead lame. So, I left him with Tom in the stables of the *château*. Poor Tom, I didn't like leaving him there all alone; but it was as safe (or dangerous) as anywhere else, and anyhow there was nothing else to be done. At the farm I met a lot of cavalry officers whom I knew, Norman N—— (since killed), K——, of the 10th Hussars, etc. A cavalry brigade had come up in support, and a little later on we saw the 10th Hussars reinforcing the fighting line most gallantly, galloping up in groups of five or six, dismounting under cover one man being left to hold *two groups* of horses sometimes and then rushing forward to the trenches.

Two N.C.O.'s of a *Zouave* regiment came over the brow of the hill behind us and said that their regiment was halted, and that their colonel wished to know whether we wanted their services. My general would not use them, but another of our generals said he would be only too pleased to do so. They were fine, bearded fellows, these two N.C.O.'s, and one of them gave me an interesting account (while they were waiting for a message) of their experiences ever since they had left Bizerta. They had helped to take over some of the British trenches on the Aisne, they told me, when our forces were withdrawn, and in this connection, they related an interesting story.

They said that a Taube had spotted that they were holding certain trenches from the fact that their red breeches showed up so conspicuously to anyone observing from above, and the report had gone in to the Germans accordingly. But the next day, for some reason or other, the khaki-clad British had once more taken over the trenches from *them*. Along came the Taube again to see whether the trenches were still held, and seeing no red, had reported them evacuated. Whereupon the German infantry came on in masses, thinking it had got an easy job, and was met by a murderous fire from the British.

At about 11 a.m. the general suddenly decided to re-transfer his headquarters to the Château Beukenhorst. I felt very glad, because I knew we should pick up Tom again. But first I was told to remain where I was, to direct all enquirers to the new place. I stayed until midday, when I mounted "Dawn" (for the last time) and rode off to the *château*.

When I got there, I handed the mare to Tom, and went to join my general. He had had a chair brought to him on the steps of the house, as the back was being shelled, and was busy dictating orders. D—— had just come in with a report, when the general started to give me a message to take to one of the brigades. He was showing me where he thought the Brigade Headquarters were on his map when D—— said, "I've just come from there, Sir; let me take it." Just at that instant the general caught sight of a mob of our men coming down the road from the enemy's direction. They were obviously stragglers, and were just clear of the Veldhoek wood, on our side of it.

"Here, I say, go and rally those men, someone!" he shouted. "Where's the provost-marshal?" There was a pause. That officer was not within earshot.

"I'll go, Sir," I said.

"Well, go quickly!" he replied, and I ran down the steps, and off across the fields.

I got to the main road, which was crowded with the stragglers, and shouted loudly to them to halt. There were shallow ditches on either side of the road, and I got them to crouch down in these. It was indeed a question whether to halt them in a line parallel to the shrapnel bursts (as now), or at right-angles to them. But as the slightest depression in the ground will tend to restore confidence, I let them be.

As other stragglers continued to come back, I had my work cut out to halt them, and soon the congestion became acute. To my question as to why they were retreating the answer invariably was that they had lost all their officers, and had no one to lead them. I walked back a bit along the line of crouching men to look for N.C.O.'s. It was then that I caught sight of our assistant provost-marshal, on the other side of the road, also engaged in stopping fugitives. I called out to him, "We must get these men on!" and I began to line them across the road, and at right-angles to it. Many of them were without rifles. The rest only wanted leading, and were quite ready to go back to the firing line. They started to advance quite gamely with me. Rifle bullets came over us in quantities, from the enemy who had gained a footing in the wood just ahead of us.

Suddenly, to my great relief, we were overtaken by successive lines of men of the 60th Rifles, advancing quickly to the attack. I called out to one of the officers to help me to take on my men, asking him if he would mind their going on with his. He said by all means, and just then, as I was looking round and shouting to them, there was a loud bang and a flash. I felt a blow on my head, and a numbing pain in my left leg. I staggered about a bit, and then fell, and was dimly conscious of other people lying about round me. Two very gallant men of the 60th ran up to me. They were indignant because the shell had been one of our own (so they said). I had crawled by now into the ditch on the side of the road. The two men gave me a drink of rum from my own flask, and bound me up with my field-dressing, after ripping up the leg of my breeches. I bled a good deal at first, and as the pain in the knee was intense, I thought it had been broken.

One of the two men told me that I had better not remain in that ditch, as the enemy were making a target of it. I said I was to be left there; but they asked me where I had just come from, for my staff cap showed that I was on some Headquarters. I said I came from the big *château* not far behind us, and they started to carry me towards it.

I was a bit muzzy from the crack on the head, and have not a very clear recollection of all that happened afterwards. I remember that just before they started to move me, I looked up and saw an officer bending over me. I recognised him at once, and said, "Hullo! aren't you W—— O——, whom I used to know at Pindi?" He said he was. The Germans, he told me, had caught his battery and killed the men and teams. They had captured two guns, and at any moment might turn them on us.

I remember soon after this finding myself clinging to a young tree that grew on the side of the road. A French *Zouave* regiment was passing me, going into action in lines of company column. I could not refrain from waving my cap to them as they passed, they had such a gallant look, and they cheered me. My two friends cannot have been far away, for very soon they were helping me back across the same field over which I had run a few minutes before being hit. "When it comes to this, there ain't much ceremony between an officer and a man," they said. Good, sterling fellows, I hope they will come safely through this war. I asked them their names, but I soon forgot what they were, alas! I think one of them was called Knott.

Shrapnel was cracking in the sky as the three of us went slowly across that interminable field. It seemed too good to be true that I was about to "get my ticket," with a wound honourably received.

We got into the *château* grounds through one of the gaps in the barbed-wire which I myself had made some days before when preparing to defend the place. Soon we were sighted by the group of officers and orderlies on the steps, and some of these ran out to help me in. I bade farewell to my two brave preservers, and was carried into the hall, and laid on a mattress. Presently the doctor and a dresser arrived and bound me up. They told me that poor D—— had been badly hit in the stomach by a piece of shell. They had taken him down below to the cellars.

I suffered pretty severe pain as I lay there. My general had gone off somewhere, but many of the other officers were about, and came and spoke to me. Among them was young N——. I sent for Tom Condon, and he fetched my saddlebag, in which were a few things that I did not want to lose. I asked him if he would like to go home now that I was hit; but he said he would "see it out." I shook hands with him, and when he had gone, I asked one of the officers to look after him. I was never to see him again.

Colonel G—— M——, our A.D.M.S., was very kind to me. He spoke most cheeringly, and said I would be back again in three weeks. I asked how the day was going, and he told me quite all right. He said a motorcar was ready to take me to hospital at Ypres; but when it came to the point, I hated the idea of leaving. I said I felt sure I should be all right again in a few days, but he was very firm, and said there was another wounded officer waiting under fire in the motor; and so, I went. As I was lifted into the car my general appeared.

"I am sorry for this, Butler," he said, as he shook hands. "But the turn of all of us will come," he added with a laugh. "Goodbye, and good luck to you, and thank you for all you have done for me!"

I asked him to keep my place open for me. My leg was covered with blood, and looking down at it he said, "You won't be coming out again."

"Oh, yes, I shall," I said, and repeated my request.

"Very well," he said, "that will be all right."

My servant, Weekes, was back at Ypres with the baggage, and so I did not see him to say goodbye.

Amidst many farewells the motor started off, and we were taken to one of the British hospitals in Ypres. The chauffeur had often driven me before, but never had I felt so indebted to him as on this occasion. It was also the very car in which the general had sent me down to the station to meet my mother when she came over to Lyndhurst from Ireland to be with me for the few days before I went out.

It was about 1.30 p.m. that I was hit, so I suppose I must have been in hospital by 4. I remember looking out of the motor to have another glimpse of the wonderful Cloth Hall as we passed through Ypres. It was intact then. We passed a French military funeral in the streets, plain black cross on the hearse and all, and then we were left at the hospital. The officers' ward was in a schoolroom, with weird and wonderful pictures on the walls of scenes from the Old Testament.

Ere night fell we were taken away again, put into one of those admirable motor-ambulances, and taken by road to Poperinghe. We kept calling to the driver to "go slowly!" for the bumping hurt us grievously. At Poperinghe we were lodged in the convent, which had been turned into a hospital. Here we were out of reach of the guns, oh, blessed thought! I was injected with anti-tetanus serum. That night I slept fairly well, though the officer in the next bed to me was very restless, poor fellow. Very early in the morning I saw a little altar being prepared and candles lighted. It was for the *Viaticum* to be administered to a dying French colonel.

Early in the morning of the 3rd November I was taken out on a stretcher, to be put into another motor-ambulance *en route* for the Poperinghe railway station. But before I left, they carried me into another ward where poor D—— lay, and put my stretcher down beside his bed. I could see he was badly wounded, but he was full of pluck and courage. He told me a shell had practically burst *on him*, as he sat on his horse. He gave me a message for his wife, and we parted. He said he was going to be all right. But he died twelve days later in Boulogne. His wife was with him at the end.

I was then taken out into the "compound," and the orderlies left me a while to myself while they went to get their rifles to shoot at a villainous Taube that was circling overhead. They said it came every morning.

After a long delay the ambulance started off for the railway station, bumping on the cobbled road quite badly. They had to saw off the handles of my stretcher before they could pass it in through the window of the train; but at last I was comfortably installed. What troubled me most was the cramp which took hold every now and then of my foot, and which I could only defeat by pressing my toes against something. Unfortunately, the seat was just too long, but another wounded officer, who occupied the opposite seat, very kindly fixed me up with a cushion.

We remained in Poperinghe railway station all that day. An angel of a nurse gave me champagne to drink (Mumm, extra *sec*, supplied free by that firm) whenever I wanted it, and I was quite happy.

The journey to Boulogne was very long, but one was so glad to be lying down that it was not tedious. We got to Boulogne and on board the *Asturias* at about 2 p.m., on the 4th November. This magnificent ship was most comfortably fitted up, and we were well cared for. There was a large officers' ward, quite full, and two or three men's wards, also packed. I believe we carried 1,100 wounded.

I had all along felt a lump at the back of my knee, and when the surgeon came to me, I told him I thought the piece of shell had lodged there. After a very cursory examination he said that this was the case, and asked me if I would like him to cut it out. I said certainly, if the matter was urgent. So, between 5.30 and 6.30 in the evening I was carried up on deck on my stretcher to the operating theatre. Of course, I did not know the degree of seriousness of my wound, and before he gave me the chloroform I asked the doctor straight out whether he was going to take my leg off! He promised me he wasn't, and the thing was soon done.

Next morning, the 5th November, greatly eased by the extraction of a small piece of shell and some breeches cloth, I wired encouragingly to my mother and sister, and at about mid-day we sailed for Southampton, where we arrived on the morning of the 6th. That same evening, I got to Guy's Hospital, where I was to remain well cared for and happy until December 2nd. My mother and eldest sister came from Ireland to be with me. My wound, although severe, was not dangerous. The piece of shell had penetrated the left thigh, just above the knee, missing a main artery by what the surgeon described as "nothing of an inch," and another piece had raised a bump on my left temple.

So, ended the first part of my experiences at the Front.

CHAPTER 15

Another Go, but Different

On Wednesday, 2nd of December, 1914 (the narrative was continued from memory at sea, sixteen months after this date—Author) exactly a month after I had received my wound in the First Battle of Ypres, I was just well enough to be discharged to a friend's house from Guy's Hospital, where I had been happy, comfortable, and well cared for. I was five and a half months at home, either on sick leave or, towards the end, on "light duty" in Dublin. Light duty soon gave way to "passed fit for general service," and on the 30th April, 1915, very suddenly, I got my orders to proceed with eight other officers of my regiment to France.

I remember that I was feeling very seedy when the news came, but the stimulus of having only three-quarters of an hour in which to pack, and to catch the mail at Westland Row, banished all unfitness. My friend G—— was coming too also for his second time and we shared a carriage.

We were not in boisterous spirits as we started off from London, though on the Kingstown to Holyhead boat the night before we had been a rowdy and hilarious enough crowd. We realised perfectly well to what sort of thing we were going back. Neuve Chapelle had taken place but a little while before, and the papers had been filled with its casualty lists, containing the names of many mutual friends. But we kept our heads high none the less, and we told each other, G—— and I, that we should move heaven and earth to get sent together to our old battalion, the 1st.

I know that G—— is now in the thick of all the fighting of the "Somme Push" in France, where, too, is my *padre* brother. God keep them safe!

From Southampton we crossed over late that night (1st May, 1915) to Havre. It was a Sunday morning when we arrived, and I remember going to Mass in a big church that looked down upon the *Place*, and that the bishop preached a sermon in which he said that the month of May, which was then opening, would see, if not the final triumph, at least a great triumph for the arms of France and her Allies. I conveyed the good news to my friends when I got out.

In Havre we met two old friends, who had each in turn been in command of the depot at Clonmel. One of them took us in the afternoon for a motor drive round the vast British standing camps upon the high ground to the north of the town, whence we could look down upon Harfleur, and where we drove through very beautiful wooded scenery. He promised, too, to do his best with the authorities in Rouen to get G—— and me posted together to the 1st Battalion. Both the 1st and 2nd Battalions we knew to be in the firing line, the 1st in the 27th Division, and the other in, I think, the 4th, and both near Ypres.

We arrived at Rouen rather late that night, to find neither porters at the station nor cabs outside. We assembled our kit, however, on the platform, and placed it in charge of a guard of French infantry (the corporal in command of which was an ill-mannered enough little creature), and then, struggling with our valises, we set out to look for an hotel.

Whether the sight of a crowd of infantry officers wearing men's equipment, and carrying their own packs, was calculated to inspire the purse-proud hotel-keepers of Rouen with mistrust, or whether their hotels really were, as they averred, full up, we were unable to gain admittance, for sleeping purposes, into either the Hotel de la Poste or the Grand Hotel du Nord. One of our party, however, knew of an officer in the A.S.C. who, he said, would either put us up or find us lodgings, and so at the Hotel du Nord we ordered the best supper that the establishment could provide, for we were famished.

It was rather curious—and to me of good omen—that this second journey to the Front should have brought me for the first night to Rouen, even as the first journey had to Bruges. These two places were the two that we had visited as children, during summer holidays years before. In Rouen we had stayed at the Grand Hotel du Nord, Rue de la Grosse Horloge—the identical spot where I found myself now, so many years afterwards, in such very different circumstances.

The young officer who had trusted to his friend in the A.S.C. had spoken the truth when he had vaunted that officer's hospitality, and in his tiny billet, in a typical Rouennais house, we all dossed down, some on sofas, some on the floor (I was one of these), and slept the sleep of utter weariness. I do not remember the name of our kind A.S.C. host, but I remember that on the mantelpiece of the room in which I slept there was a photograph of his brother, killed in the Mons retreat. Even then it was an everyday thing to come upon someone who had suffered a near bereavement.

The one officer's servant on the premises had a busy time next morning with hot water. I was the first up, for I wanted to go out early to the cathedral. What a sight it was, when from a side street I came suddenly on that masterpiece! Nothing in nature can produce quite the feeling with which one regards the teeming beauty of a French cathedral's *façade*. And there was the Tour de Beurre, lit by the morning sunshine, and bringing back to me so poignantly the days of my boyhood's visit, its enthusiasm, and its very dear companionships.

The British Army camp was situated on high ground some miles out of the town, to the south; and thither we soon repaired, to report, and to learn our destination. G—— and I kept together, and went to the 27th Divisional Camp, where we were to remain for three or four days. When we had been there about a day O'C—— arrived, too, with a draft from home. In the end G—— and I were posted to the 1st Battalion, and O'C—— to the 2nd.

The camp was overcrowded and uncomfortable, and all three of us managed to be away from it during most of the time, and to get into the town of Rouen.

Having always had a great reverence and enthusiasm for Joan of Arc, I had, as soon as I heard that we were bound for Rouen, determined to lay a wreath at the foot of her statue in the Place la Pucelle, as a token of homage. O'C——, who was always full of adventure, and brimming over with life and the joy thereof, was enthusiastically in favour of the proposition, which I had broached to him and G——. They said they would both share the cost, whatever it might be; but they insisted that I was to "run the show" from beginning to end.

O'C—— pretended that he expected at least the Cross of the *Légion d'Honneur* out of it, and boisterously insisted that I should see that the municipal authorities were furnished with our exact names, addresses, and parentage! "Besides," said he, "it will bring me luck. Joan is my wife's name. It *must* bring me luck!"

Poor fellow, in three weeks' time he was to be dead—gassed by those fiends of Germans.

But all things were equally possible to all of us then, and it was no use looking gloomily ahead. I at once set about making arrangements with regard to the wreath. One morning, while the others were in camp, I obtained leave to visit the town. I knew that I should first have to obtain the permission of the mayor, or of the chief civil functionary, whoever he might be. So, I repaired to the Hotel de Ville, and after a great deal of explanation, of shoulder-shrugging, and of being passed on from one department to another, I found myself in the presence of the *sous-maire*, the mayor himself not being at home. The *sous-maire* took me to the Architect-in-Chief of Rouen, a gentleman encased in a tight-fitting frock coat, with tall hat and black gloves (it was a hot day).

I explained again to him that I, and two other officers of my regiment, craved permission to place a *couronne de fleurs* at the foot of the statue of Joan of Arc in the Place la Pucelle. The act was to be a purely private one, I said; and this assurance seemed to give him and the *sous-maire* satisfaction. After a hurried consultation between the two, the chief architect jumped up from his green baize table, and seizing his hat, gloves, and stick, bade me follow him. We walked together to a little flower shop in one of the main streets, where we explained our scheme to the delighted woman behind the counter. She quite understood, she said. She would make me a magnificent *couronne* of roses and lilies, and tie it with broad silken ribands, in the French and English colours.

My architect friend was become most enthusiastic, and later on, when the *couronne* was ready, he returned with me (having meanwhile been to measure the height from the ground to the base of the statue), borrowed a ladder and a youth from the shop, and together we sallied forth to perform the little act of homage. The crown was a magnificent one; but the architect, who had enquired of me the price I had paid for it, told me confidentially as we went that I had paid too much.

We were followed down the street by many curious glances, but before a crowd had had time to collect, we had fixed the crown in position, high up on the front of the pedestal. I had attached to it a card on which was written:

De la part de trois officiers irlandais.

My friend and I then took some refreshment together in a *café*, and we parted, though not before he had extracted from me a few details that afterwards went to the making of a paragraph in the Rouen papers, and a promise that should I ever be in the town again I should go and visit him at his home. He was an excellent fellow. Later on, O'C—— and G—— drove through the *Place*, and had a look at the crown of flowers. "*Cet hommage,*" *dit l'un d'eux* (I remember the paragraph in the papers ended up), "*nous portera bonheur.*"

Rouen was, of course, crowded with British officers and men. In fact, the British Army seemed to have taken over the town in everything but name. All the little tables in front of the chief restaurants along the quay were occupied by khaki-clad figures, and it made us rage to see how completely the smartness and the spick-and-spanness which we of the Old Army had always loved and cultivated had disappeared. Our people compared badly with the French, and this was not only because they had a less becoming uniform, but their whole appearance and turn-out were slipshod and untidy. There were exceptions, of course, but this was the general rule.

We left Rouen for the north on about the 5th of May, on a glorious spring evening. I shall never forget the view we got as we steamed slowly out across the iron railway-bridge and saw the spire and towers of the cathedral against the sunset sky. One so often in wartime refuses to let the mind register impressions, lest they be too much for one's equanimity—to dwell upon beauty of land, or sea, or sky—to think of one's dear ones. But every now and then there comes some wondrous thing that will not be denied. Such a one was this river-reflected vision of Rouen's towers and sunset.

This was, as I have said, about the 5th of May. The 7th was my regimental birthday. It seemed pretty certain that I was to spend this anniversary under fire. Somehow or other we heard as we travelled up that the famous Hill 60, over the taking of which by the British there had been much exulting just prior to our departure, had been re-wrested from us by the Germans. We were told (though this did not materialise in our case) that we were to pass over a portion of the line that was regularly shelled by the enemy's big guns. We knew that we were bound for the apex of the Ypres salient.

We had a fairly comfortable night, and a well-stocked luncheon-basket, which we had obtained at Rouen. At the then railhead, a little place called Caestre, we detrained. I had been put in charge of a draft of about two hundred men for the Rifle Brigade, and a better behaved lot of fellows it would be impossible to find. This draft, and several others, assembled in a field near the station, and after a short rest we crowded on and into a long row of motor-buses that were to take us up to our various regimental headquarters.

This means of transport appeared to me, after what I had been through in the First Ypres, to be dangerous in the extreme, and I must admit that as I sat there in a front seat of the leading bus, I expected every moment that we should get shelled. Later on, how I should have laughed at imagining a spot as far back as *this* dangerous!

Just before we started off a regiment of British cavalry passed us. The men were alert and well set up, and their horses in the pink of condition. This was to be practically the last I saw of cavalry, *qu'à* cavalry, until I left France, nearly six months later.

We may have been a dozen motor-buses in all, with about forty officers and men to each bus. There was about fifteen yards between each vehicle, and at the head of all rode a young A.S.C. officer on a motor-bicycle. We were to go to some cross-roads near a hamlet called Busseboom, and our route lay through Poperinghe, the place where I had lain for a night after being wounded.

The young A.S.C. officer led us well, and we were not shelled. The sound of the big guns was in our ears throughout all that day. Poperinghe, as we passed through it, bore many evidences of the shelling which it had received from time to time, and was mostly deserted by its inhabitants. Some distance to the east of the town we struck off from the main road to the right, and after a while the buses came finally to a full stop, and we got out. I soon disposed of my draft, and was at liberty to go in search of our Battalion Headquarter camp, whither G—— and the others had already gone.

The Headquarter camp of a battalion in the trenches is not to be confounded with Battalion Headquarters, which latter are practically up in the trenches too. At the Headquarter camp—usually some three or four miles back from the front-line trenches—are to be found the quartermaster, chaplain, transport officer, quartermaster-sergeant, transport, etc., etc. From here the transport, with rations, letters, R.E. stores, etc., moves up every evening, at about dusk, to the "Dump," which is generally situated close to Battalion Headquarters. The Headquarter camp is thus the first thing actually of the battalion that one meets with on one's way from the base to the firing line, and is the spot where officers and drafts collect and rest for a brief spell, before entering the fray.

I had not seen the battalion since the summer of 1912, when I had been ordered home from India for a tour of duty at the Regimental Depot. It was, therefore, especially in the circumstances, a joy to come upon familiar faces. The quartermaster was an old friend of my Indian days. Many, too, of the transport men were known to me, and it was nice to hear their brogues.

There was a pleasant surprise in store for me. "Lodestar," one of my old ponies, was there. She had come on from India with the regiment, and was now the quartermaster's charger. As soon as I heard of her, I went with all speed to where she was stabled, in a cowshed of Busseboom Farm, and the dear old mare knew me, and whinnied as I entered.

Halcyon Indian racing days came back to me during the few minutes that I spent in "Lodestar's" box, in the gloaming of that Flemish farmstead. I forgot for a while the booming of the guns outside, and the business which I had in hand. But my thoughts were dreadfully lonely ones. For, even at that period of the war, what a number of tried old friends and rivals of those glorious Indian days were gone!

CHAPTER 16

Ypres Again

The morrow was not, after all, to be spent in the firing line. On three sides of us, at distances varying from four miles to eight, the battle raged most furiously, and orders came that we were not to attempt to go up for the present. So, for about two days we remained at the Busseboom Farm, sleeping in some bell-tents that had been pitched for us near the buildings, and taking our meals in the farmhouse. The younger officers amused themselves by kicking a football about, while G—— and I mostly wrote letters. O'C—— turned up suddenly, having ridden over from the Headquarter camp of the 2nd Battalion, which was not far away, and where he was similarly situated to us. I had a few words with him. He sat there on his horse in his old inimitable way. Of course, he had a hunting-crop, with a long lash, which he loudly cracked from time to time. I never saw him afterwards.

At last it was definitely decided that we were to go up—all nine of us—to the trenches with the rations that night, 7th May. Having said goodbye to the chaplain and the quartermaster, and with many wishes of "Good luck" from them, we set off, while it was still broad daylight. We were convoyed by the transport officer (who performed this journey, and return, most gallantly every night, and who afterwards got the Military Cross for his good work), I riding my dear old "Lodestar." For a time, all went well. Our road led us through Vlamertinghe, and the nearest thing that came to us in the way of shelling was an occasional hiss and clatter as a missile from a German long-range gun came flying over us into the unfortunate Poperinghe.

It was extraordinarily difficult not to believe that this gun was fired from the middle of a thicket close at hand. The fact that the report of the discharge and the report of the explosion of the shell were very close together was responsible for this. Several times during the day we had been on the point of crossing over to explore the thicket, and circumstantial tales were put about of German spies having remained with a gun buried in a cunningly-concealed dug-out in the wood, etc., etc. As a matter of fact, this particular gun was being fired from some position far behind the German lines.

After a long, slow ride, just as it was beginning to grow dusk, and while we were yet a couple of miles or so short of Ypres, we turned off the high road, away from the familiar *pavé*, and struck off to the right, along a softer road. All that I could see of poor ruined Ypres was a jagged corner of the Cloth Hall tower above the trees. I did not like to look, and like Richard Coeur de Lion (although my heart was feeling anything but that of a lion at the time) I turned away.

At a certain spot, which must have been on the road to Zillebeke, of stirring memory (but how weird and unreal seemed all these places to me now, in my altered circumstances!), we were told to dismount. The horses were to be sent back, and we were to perform the remainder of our journey to the trenches in single-file on foot.

From this point on, the night was like a bad dream. It was pretty dark by now, and the shelling had begun in earnest. I remember that we entered the outskirts of Ypres by a circuitous route, that we crossed over the canal by a bridge, and that then we struck off to the east along a railway embankment. The embankment was pitted with shell-holes, and in places the rails had been torn up, twisted, and thrown on one side by the force of the explosions. We moved steadily along in single-file, and after a good deal of stumbling and falling about we got into a fairly deep cutting. It was probably not at this, but at a wood just to the left of it, in which was one of our batteries, that the Germans were firing; but shell after shell came screaming up to us from the east, and bursting all around.

We ducked as one man when we heard these shells coming, and humped our backs in the most approved style so as to get the maximum amount of protection from the heavy packs which we were carrying. Very few of us said anything, with the exception of a garrulous and quite irrepressible Irishman from Galway, who kept up a running fire of "bad cesses," "the mischief take it," and the like, punctuated by laughs, and who certainly provided the comic relief of the entertainment.

One thing occurred, I remember, which gave our friend more cause for amusement than anything else. I did not see it: I only heard his laughter. We were moving in order of seniority, so that I was going

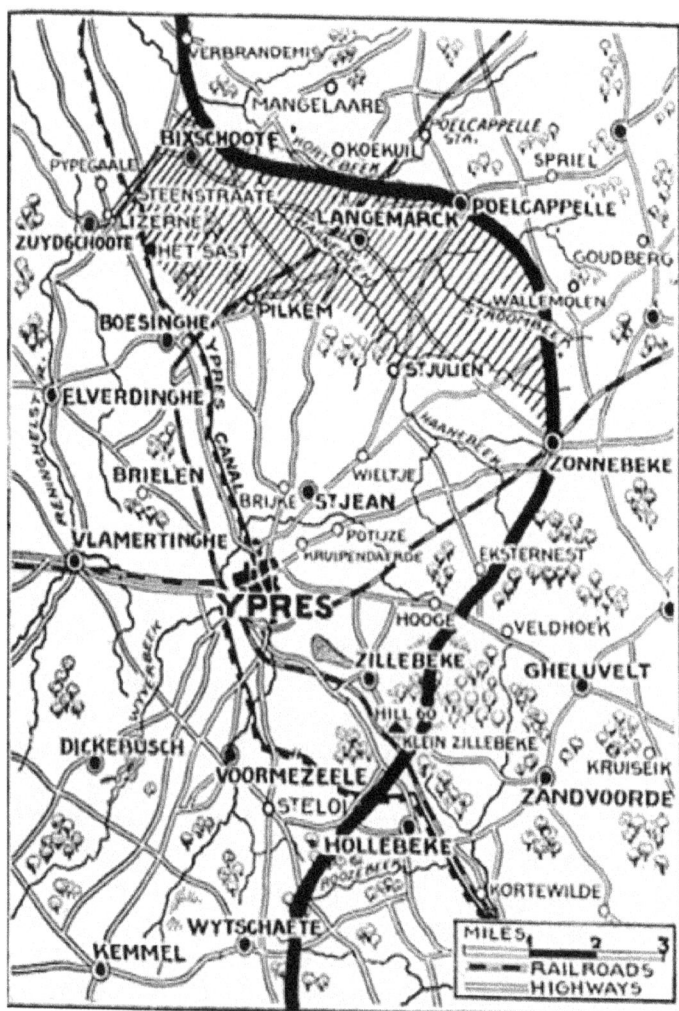

The 2nd Battle of Ypres

second, and he was nearly last. One of the party was a very good fellow, named P—— who had been out before, and who on the strength of this had offered to be of assistance to the man from Galway by going in front of him and allowing him to catch hold of his pack for guidance. This having been agreed to, P—— promptly proceeded to fall into a shell-hole, and the man from Galway had to haul him out! So sudden a reversal of their intended roles was too much for Galway, and for the remainder of that march he did nothing but crow and chuckle.

As we got nearer the trenches the sky grew brighter with flares—things which had not been in use when I was out before, but with which I was very soon to grow familiar. We gained some knowledge of the desperate nature of the salient we were in by seeing, whenever we looked round, how almost completely the double line of flares—ours and the enemy's—encircled us. It looked as though the narrow strip of ground that gave access to the salient must be pinched in before long. But it was not pinched in in our time, nor has it been so yet.

After what seemed interminable marching we got into a wood, which we were told was the beginning of Sanctuary Wood, and having arrived at the "Dump" we were taken in charge by guides, who were to lead us up to Battalion Headquarters. The shelling had practically ceased now, but a good deal of sniping was going on. We made our way carefully forward, and at length arrived in a part of the wood that seemed to be in a hollow, and where there were several dug-outs. It was very dark. We halted outside one of the largest dug-outs. Somebody knocked at the door, and a voice from inside bade us enter.

The whole nine of us crowded into the dug-out, which was a shelter built of stout wooden piles, with a mud floor, and a roof, also of piles, that was thickly covered with earth. The interior must have been about twenty feet by twelve. One end of it was entirely filled by a large bed, looted, no doubt, from some private house nearby. There was also a small table, a stove, and some chairs. On a heap of straw at the foot of the bed was a cat with a litter of kittens. The walls were damp, and the whole place smelt of mould.

In this dug-out (it appeared palatial to us later on) were three people. One was C——, the adjutant, whom I had long known, and the other two were strangers to me. They were the commanding officer and the doctor.

One after another we were introduced to the C.O. by the adjutant. No time was lost in talk. We were informed that the battalion had had a bad day in the trenches, and that we were wanted up there at once.

So, the telling-off to companies began. "Captain G——," said the adjutant, "you will be second-in-command, and remain here." (Lucky G——!)

"Captain Butler," he continued, "you will take over 'C' Company. (A pause.) And you'll get hell!"

This promised to be a rude introduction to trench warfare. From the N.C.O. of the ration party, with which I was to go up to the trenches, I learnt that the trench which "C" Company was holding had been "blown in" in several places that day; that is, that it had been so heavily shelled by high explosive that it had partially collapsed. About a score of men had been buried in the ruins, and of these not all had been recovered alive. But I also learnt that the company was to be relieved the following night.

To the east of Sanctuary Wood, the ground rose rapidly for a distance of about 150 or 200 yards, and just a little way over the crest were our front-line trenches, and then, about 400 yards further on, the German lines. To get to my trench one took advantage of the cover from view which was afforded by this rise, and moved along on the surface. Just before one reached the crest-line, however, the communication-trench began, and from there onwards one twisted along through ankle-deep mud in the general direction of the front-line trenches. In the ordinary trench that was in good repair (such as we found later on in other parts of the line) one could walk upright without, as a rule, exposing oneself to the enemy's snipers.

But these Sanctuary Wood trenches had been constructed in a hurry, and moreover they had been "blown in" very often, with the result that in places—sometimes for twenty yards at a time—one had to stoop very low to avoid being seen. It was dark, of course, but every now and then a flare would go up, either from the German trenches or from our own, and at such times one would imagine the surroundings to have become as clear as day. As a matter of fact, provided a man remains still while a flare is up, even though he may be in the open, the chances are that he will not be seen. One soon got to realise this; but just at first one was naturally a bit extra careful.

There was not much traffic in the communication-trench on this night, and in spite of atrocious mud I was not long in arriving at the front-line trench. I was taken to the fire-bay that did duty as Company Headquarters in those very elementary trenches (elementary, that is, according to my subsequent knowledge, but to me at the time appearing solid enough), and there I found the subaltern who had been in command of the company during the preceding weeks. It was too dark to distinguish faces, but the subaltern was possessed of a cheery Irish brogue, and he was of the sort that at once inspires confidence. In spite of all he had been through that day, and many others, he was cheeriness itself, as he showed me round the narrow domain that was to be my command—the tiny, but vital, sector of England's front line of defence.

It took me only a very short time to become acquainted with the routine of ordinary trench warfare, and to settle down to it. It was just as well, perhaps, that the life was not difficult to become accustomed to, for in my role of veteran of First Ypres I had to appear as though well inured to it. In point of fact, however, nothing could have been more different from my first experience of warfare than this second phase that had now begun for me. Then, it had all been above-ground work for me, with much galloping about and a great deal of movement. Now, it was a matter of remaining tied to a deep, narrow pit in the ground, herded chock-a-block with one's fellow men, and seeing nothing at all of the surrounding country.

But although I had known during the march up to the wood that we were somewhere not very far away from ground that must have been familiar to me, yet it was not without a sense of surprise and incredulity that I discovered some days later that my trench was dug in a hill that I had often ridden over in the first battle, that the farm where we had had our Divisional Headquarters at the end of October and the beginning of November must be only about eight hundred yards away in front of me, and that the big ruined building away to the left front, which one could just distinguish through the periscope, was the once spick-and-span Beukenhorst Castle, in which we had lived for so long.

On the day that I was wounded (2nd November) our line had gone back to my "little black-and-white village" of Hooge. This was away on our left now, hidden by the wooded slopes whereon I had seen the *Chasseurs* and the 10th Hussars mustering for their attacks, and it was still in our possession. Yes, it was indeed strange to be looking out now (mostly through a periscope) at the ground that our Immortal Seventh Division had consecrated with its blood, which was the scene of all my hopes and fears, doubts and resolves, lonely rides and hazards, and to be back again as a regimental instead of as a staff officer, with the German front line on the ground that had then been in rear of ours.

My first night in the trenches turned out, fortunately, to be a quiet one. I was able to get a little sleep, stretched on the narrow fire-step, and I was dog-tired. In those trenches there were no dug-outs, such as we subsequently found in other parts of the line. Officers and men, when they were not on duty, simply lay down as best they could on the fire-step, the only concession to officers being that they generally had one or two fire-bays exclusively set apart for them and their servants. In case of attack the servants would go to their platoons, and the captain to where he was most required.

The British always seemed to make far more use of sandbags than did the French. These Sanctuary Wood trenches were no exception to the rule. The top of the parapet was hardly ever flush with the level of the ground, there being as a rule two or three courses of sandbags on top of the interior "slope," which, of course, was sheer. There were traverses at about every five yards, and both fire-step and parapet were generally revetted by means of brushwood or wire, supported by stout stakes. The fire-step was just broad enough to permit of a man lying down on it, while the sentries maintained their ceaseless vigil in the corners of the bays.

Sniping, both from the enemy's side and from our own, went on all that night, and a few shells flew over us and the wood in rear. When day dawned, I was able to take better stock of my command, and even to pay flying visits to the trenches on my right and left. I found several old friends, and the day passed quickly enough.

After nightfall our relief by another company took place, and we stumbled out, in long files, and then formed up in the wood in rear, near the Battalion Headquarters dug-out. My first tour of the trenches was happily over, and I had scarcely had a casualty. The men crawled into more or less splinter-proof dug-outs that were dotted about in the wood, and we, the company officers, did the same. I remember it was close on midnight when we were at last able to throw ourselves down, utterly weary, on some damp and evil-smelling straw. I only troubled to remove my boots and coat, and wrapping myself in my British Warm (our valises containing our blankets had had to be left behind at Busseboom), I fell into a sound sleep, from which I did not awaken until the day was well advanced.

Things were at that period so unsettled that the most that the relieved company could get was about eighteen hours in *demi-repos*. We would accordingly have to go up into the trenches again that night, and so for the little time of rest at our disposal we mostly slept, or at least lay on, in our blankets until the afternoon.

When I did at length crawl out of the dug-out, which I had shared with two other officers, and was able to take a look round, it was a strange sight that greeted me. The whole environment of that dug-out, under those conditions, was indescribably eerie and unnatural. To try and put it in a few words, it was as though one stood in the presence of the Day of Judgment, while Nature had for some unaccountable reason *not stopped*. For in that torn, twisted and uprooted wood the birds were singing and the trees were coming into leaf. The sun was sending its lifegiving rays slanting down the rides, and a tiny brook ran tinkling beneath the rustic bridge that gave access to our dug-out. But bullets were flying through the trees, and every now and then a shell would shriek into them, while to taste of the brook meant death, for it had long been full of dead. This glaring discrepancy between Man and Nature made one feel strangely friendless and alone.

The days and nights that followed made up a period that it would be difficult to write about in detail, but that formed one continual time of high pressure and anxiety. Although all the casualties, save four, that I saw occur took place in the trenches, and not in the wood in rear, yet the life in the latter was by far the most difficult to endure. In the trenches one at least had the feeling of being in action, even if one never saw an enemy. But in the *demi-repos* wood one pretended to be in security, or rather one gambled on the chance of it. When you left your dug-out to visit your men, or for any other reason, you chanced a bullet, or the sudden visitation of an all-crushing shell. The dug-outs themselves would all have been flattened out by a direct hit from a shell, and were at best only splinter-proof. In the fortnight that I spent in the Sanctuary Wood position I came out of the trenches about three times, for about eighteen hours at a time, and generally the hours between dusk and the return to the trenches were occupied in digging drains or repairing the damage done to the communication-trenches by shells.

The battalion was responsible for three trenches, each one being held by a company, which permitted of one company being out each night. Somehow or other the long hours in the trenches passed quickly. One got one's letters up with the rations every evening, and when one was not being shelled or otherwise kept busy there was always opportunity for a quiet read in one's fire-bay. An exceedingly cold snap visited the trenches in the middle of May that year, and the nights were bitter. One lived on bully beef, supplemented by such comforts as were sent out from home, and the cooking was of the most elementary description, done in little recesses cut in the bottom of the parados. When it rained, as it often did, one tried to keep the water from running down the back of one's neck by rigging up a waterproof sheet over the fire-step. Then, if a shell struck anywhere in the vicinity one was covered from head to foot with mud, instead of sand, as was the case in dry weather.

The shell most usually employed against us was the "*whizbang*," so called from the incredibly sudden way in which the explosion and the noise of passing would occur, there being no time to move before the whole thing was over and done with. It was a small shell, and rarely did any particular damage, though it frequently sent a load of sandbags from the top of the parapet down upon one's head, which would come very near to stunning one.

Some of the subalterns in my trench had good voices, and sometimes at night they used to sing part-songs together, which sounded very well. There was in particular one young fellow, a native of Cork, who had a beautiful voice; and if ever, even now, I hear any of his songs being sung or played it brings me back again in spirit to those weird days of stress and anxiety, of kindliness and *camaraderie*, the long watches of the night, the cup of refreshing cocoa, the desultory rifle fire, the chill of dawn, and the daily stirring into life of the bird world. At the first streak of dawn the skylarks used to sing themselves steadily up into the pale sky, pouring their little souls out with a joy that was strangely out of keeping with our life.

It was this subaltern of the beautiful voice; who used to read a few prayers over the men we were able to bury, and the company loved him for it. The harshest tones soothe at such a time; but when you have the gentle South of Ireland accent added to a charming voice, and reading the Burial Service, I think the limit of which human words are capable is reached. (This officer, Captain O'Brien, was afterwards killed in the Holy Land, while leading his men in the attack—Author.)

It must not be supposed that we were ever anything approaching the lugubrious in the trenches, even when things were at their worst. In the worst bits of trench the officers used often to stick up humorous notices, and I remember one corner especially, a very narrow one round a traverse, that was labelled:

It is easier for a camel to pass through the eye of a needle than

134

for a fat man to pass this corner.

There was a certain fire-bay that was placarded with notices to the effect that it was the happy hunting-ground of "Fritz," but here, unfortunately, a very distressing accident occurred.

A gunner major, tired of remaining with his battery, far in rear, and letting his subaltern perform the duties of forward observation officer, decided one day to reverse the roles. He would observe the result of his battery's fire from the front-line trenches, while his subaltern would direct the fire in accordance with his orders in rear. In spite of all the warnings of the officers of another company of my regiment, who were on the spot, the major insisted upon observing from the dangerous bit of trench. What was more, prior to adjusting the periscope with which his orderly was furnished, he deliberately stood up on the fire-step and surveyed the enemy's trenches. He paid for his *nonchalance* with his life. There was the sudden, mysterious crack of a striking bullet. It had got him clean through one eye, and he fell dead without a word.

That very morning this same major had most kindly left a box of cigarettes for me at the Headquarters dug-out. My company was out of the trenches that day.

It would only weary if I were to attempt to recount in detail the events of those long days in the Sanctuary Wood trenches. I should like, though, to put on record my gratitude for the fact that the period of my holding the command of "C" Company, both then and afterwards, coincided with the company's greatest immunity from casualties. I also bear willing tribute to the coolness, pluck, and good temper of an admirable lot of men.

CHAPTER 17

From Second Ypres to Armentières

I find the following entry in my notebook, under date 18th May: *Lost ring*. I had a very beautifully engraved signet ring that had belonged to my father, and to which I naturally attached great value. It was a little bit loose for my finger, and there had always been the danger of its slipping off unknown to me. We had had a particularly wretched time coming out of the trenches on relief the night before, the mud being incredibly deep and clinging. I had arrived tired out at my dug-out, and thrown myself down to sleep on the damp straw that formed the nightly bed of the officers of one or the other company. In the morning I was sent for by the colonel, and it was not until I had finished my interview with him that I noticed that the ring was no longer on my finger.

The loss of the ring was a blow, and affected me deeply. When one loses something that has been with one right through the mill, and that has other and deeper sentimental values attached to it, the loss may very easily appear a thing of ill-omen. I went back to the dug-out and got my servant to help me in turning out the straw. Then I searched all the ground between my dug-out and Battalion Headquarters. But all my efforts were only in the nature of a very forlorn hope, for on thinking things over I remembered that I had several times fallen in coming out of the trenches overnight, and that in my efforts to save myself I had plunged my hands into the thick mud. Most probably the ring had been sucked off my finger, and was now a couple of feet below the surface of the ground. I had to go back to the trenches that night, and so gave up the search.

On about the 20th May very heavy shelling by the enemy began, coming from a point on our right front (as far as I could judge), and directed against the 28th Division's part of the line, upon the Menin road. Never had I heard more persistent shelling of one point, and with absolutely no reply from our guns. It began at the first streak of dawn, and continued without intermission for many hours. It really was most extraordinary to hear the almost continuous swish of the big projectiles as they passed over our heads in steady flow. They seemed all to keep the self-same path in the sky, and so persistent were they that they must have made a current of air in the direction of their travel. One felt so helpless, sitting there in our trenches while this wind of death swept down upon the devoted division on our left. We knew that it predicted a big assault upon the line, and afterwards we learnt that it had heralded the great attack which formed the Second Battle of Ypres.

On about May 21st the glad news reached us that we were to go back to Busseboom for a well-needed rest, but several times later on the rumour was contradicted. Things had been going very hard away on our left, and it is no harm to say now that a general retirement of the whole line to a new position some miles in rear was in contemplation. Then secret orders were issued dealing with a situation that might at any moment arise, in which a mere skeleton covering-force was to be left to hold the trenches in Sanctuary Wood, while the remainder of our force got away. In our part of the line half a company was the unit chosen for this job, and that half company was to be found by me; and, naturally, I should have commanded it.

Had this scheme been carried out I should probably not have been alive to write these lines. But fortunately, the 28th Division line held, and the original idea of our relief in the normal way could now be put into execution.

On the night of the 22nd May we were relieved by a battalion of the York and Lancasters. The relief took place by companies, and instructions were issued to each company commander that he was to march his men, on relief, down to an open space near the "Dump," and there form up in column, and lie down. It was a very dark night, and the companies arrived at the rendezvous at different intervals. My company was there second, and shortly afterwards another one arrived, moving in ghostly silence down to the appointed spot. But the 4th Company, which was now in charge of a young and rather inexperienced officer, kept us all waiting for nearly two hours. I knew that it was essential that we should get away before dawn, and, indeed, the adjutant had told me confidentially that the route we were going to take would bring us at a certain point full in view of the enemy's artillery observers on Hill 60.

Guides and messengers were, of course, sent off to find the missing company. How we all cursed it as we lay there in the open, waiting! If the enemy had had the slightest inkling of what was taking place, he would have plastered the place of our rendezvous with shell, and it would have been an ugly business. As the minutes slipped by the tension became great. Luckily, however, though many flares went up from the trenches we had handed over (enough to show the Germans that they had a fresh lot in front of them), we were not discovered. Many stray bullets flew over us, and every now and then there was a hiss and "*phut*" as one struck the ground nearby. We had three men hit, but I do not think that anyone was killed.

At last the missing company arrived, its commander full of excuses. It was the old story. He had come upon a halted body of troops, and blindly taking his cue from them, had halted too.

However, better late than too late; and we started off, heading in the direction of the southwestern outskirts of Ypres. The pace was very slow, for the men were heavily laden, and the six long weeks which they had spent in the front-line trenches had not improved their marching powers. We cut across country at various points, and day had just begun to dawn when we passed the spot that was visible from Hill 60. It must still have been too dark, down in the misty hollow where we marched, for the enemy to see us; but I could see the fatal hill quite plainly, as it stood quietly up against the lightening sky.

We passed through patches of reedy marsh, and over fields lying fallow, and as we moved along in file on the far side of a railway embankment, we saw how it was honeycombed with the dugouts and emplacements of our outgunned and outnumbered artillery. A most sweet spring morning was stealing over the scarred world as we passed by a suburb of poor Ypres. This time I could look upon those battered walls more steadily. I had struck another blow in their defence, and our line still held.

Nothing could exceed the beauty of the day breaking over the rose-red city, for rose-red it looked in that wonderful morning light. The very ruin of its matchless buildings had lent to it a new charm and marvel. The young budding orchards that we saw through a great rent in a convent wall were good to look upon, in spite of their desertedness, and all that it meant.

By now the men had begun to flag, and it took us all our time to get them along. Just as we had begun to think that a long halt was inevitable, our eyes were greeted by the sight of some twenty travel-stained motor-buses, drawn up on the side of the road. It seemed too good to be true; but they *were* for us, and they were to take us a considerable distance along our road. It only remained for the men to be told off to them in batches, and off we set, I myself finding a seat beside the driver of one of them, where I promptly fell asleep.

When I awoke, we were rolling easily along between banks of lilac and may, and the air was full of a freshness indescribable. Ah! but it was good to be alive. Nature was no longer aloof, detached. She was our friend, ours as men and Britons; and the magic of her youth ran tingling through our veins.

At the spot where the motors halted, and we descended to form up for our march into camp, we found ponies waiting for the Company Commanders, and once more I was able to be in the saddle. We marched to the very fields of Busseboom which we had quitted a fortnight before, and as we filed in through the gate the brigadier stood by the side of the road and watched us pass. Each company formed up along a boundary hedge, and the men removed their equipment and set about lighting fires and making tea. The officers were given accommodation in the farm buildings and in tents, with quantities of fresh, sweet-smelling straw to lie on.

The 23rd May was a day of uninterrupted rest for us, though the very heavy gunfire that broke out during the morning, and lasted all that day and the next, was ominous. Very early in the morning of the 24th, as I still lay snugly in my straw, I heard the adjutant calling loudly for the sergeant-major. "The battalion to be ready to move at half an hour's notice!" was his order (he really said "in half an hour"). I got up and dressed hurriedly, and as I did so I felt a great smarting in the eyes that I was unable to account for. Then other people began to complain of the same thing. It was due to traces of the enemy's big gas attack in front of Ypres, and, though we did not know about it till long after, at that moment our 2nd Battalion was being suffocated and driven back, and poor O'C——, the gay and debonair, had met his death.

That day was a radiantly fine one. When I had finished dressing, I started to help my servant to put my kit in order. My haversack needed shaking out, as it had accumulated a fair amount of crumbs, etc., after all those days. I plunged my hand down into its depths, and in a corner, I came upon my ring. It must have dropped from my finger when I pulled my hand out of the mud that night and fallen into the haversack that hung by my side. After that I felt confident that even if we had to go back, all would be well. As a matter of fact, we did not have to go back. One brigade of our division went up, and another went part of the way; but we were left in peace. We remained in a state of suspense all that day, but by nightfall the noise of battle had quietened down considerably. We were able to put in another good night's rest, and early on the morning of the 25th we marched to a little place called Locre. There we bivouacked in a field that was bordered with huge elms, and in the middle of which was a pond.

The band of a Kitchener battalion met us outside the village and played us through it: a graceful act that put us all into good humour. In the afternoon the band turned up again, and played a selection of music in our bivouac field, consisting mainly of Irish airs. It was a perfect day, and a mail had arrived from home. G—— and I found a secluded spot in the hedge, where we lay reading our letters, writing answers to them, and listening to the band. It was indeed a change after all we had been through. I remember how the lazy peacefulness of it crept into my letters, and how impressed G—— pretended to be at one passage that I read to him about "reedy ponds in which the dreamy Flemish cattle stood."

Later in the evening I went off to the village, and into the little church for Benediction. It was full of British soldiers and Flemish women and children. The familiar, simple service had never been more impressive than it was that evening, in this tiny village of the last-remaining strip of Belgium that could call its soul its own.

I slept out in the field with my company that night, wrapped in my trusty Jaeger blanket, and was up at 4 o'clock next morning, the 26th May, for at a quarter to five we were to continue our march in the direction of Bailleul.

My company was the last one to move off that morning, and having started them I rode back to the place of our encampment to see that it had been left clean, and that the "sanitary party" were doing their work. I found them engaged in assiduously burying an enormous number of unopened bully beef tins, which the men (always disgracefully wasteful of their rations) had thrown away. I remonstrated, asking that it might at least be left unburied for the inhabitants. I was told that a very stringent regulation existed to the effect that no rations were on any account ever to be made over to civilians, and that they were to be burnt or buried rather than this. I interviewed the adjutant, and obtained from him an order that the burial of all this good food should cease; and as soon as we had left the place, I have no doubt that the local children swooped down and took it all away to their homes. I remember noting the exact time that morning that we crossed the frontier into France——five minutes past five. It was still early as we passed through Bailleul. The men were in fine form, and swung gaily through the wide, cobbled streets of the town.

We pushed on a good many miles beyond Bailleul, and came to a halt at a little village called Le Petit Mortier. My company was billeted in a ramshackle, deserted schoolhouse, and the C.O. (as was his kindly custom) asked me to share the Battalion Headquarter Mess, and gave me permission to billet in the same house as the chaplain. I was at that time the only company commander with any service, and (largely owing, I am sure, to G——'s good offices) I was always treated with great consideration.

I was not to get much sleep that night. Up to then we had been quite ignorant of our destination, but it had been pretty well taken for granted that we were going back "somewhere" for a prolonged rest. Hardly, however, were we settled into Le Petit Mortier when the C.O. and all the company commanders were summoned to Brigade Headquarters, which had been established in an inn on the road to Steenwerck and Armentières. I got the summons just as I arrived back at the hamlet from a stroll of discovery with G——.

We had examined some old trenches in the vicinity, and returned down a beautiful shady track that led along by the bank of a stream. All of a sudden, not far from our path, there was a dull roar, and a great column of smoke and earth rose up into the sky. We took it to be a "Jack Johnson" that the enemy had fired at long range. Later on, however, we heard that it was an explosion at an experimental bomb school that had been started at that spot. Several people had been killed by it, including a general who was riding past at the time.

On receipt of the message ordering me to repair to Brigade Head-quarters I immediately sent for my pony, and very soon I was in the general's presence. We were told that the division was about to take over the Armentières trenches (in our case from the 19th Brigade), and that certain selected officers from each battalion were to go that afternoon by motor-bus to view these trenches.

Two buses took the lot of us. We passed through the little towns of Steenwerck, which was gay with French flags, and Nieppe, and entered Armentières from the west. It seemed a thriving place; but we had not much time to look about before we were cruising along a rather battered street, almost within view of the German lines. It then transpired that our drivers had only the very vaguest idea of where they were to take us. An annoying little officer in a Burberry (which made it impossible to recognise his rank) had been giving directions; but now that we had blundered almost into the German lines, or at any rate a long way further than motor vehicles were ever allowed to go, he admitted his entire ignorance of the locality, and so I took it upon myself to halt the buses, and prosecute inquiries on foot. At a certain Brigade Headquarters we discovered that our bus should have gone to a point called "Motorcar Corner," on another side of the town, while the second bus should have gone somewhere else.

We arrived at our destination safely in the end, and were then taken in hand by guides. They took us up along some communication-trenches that were as the corridors of palaces after what we had become accustomed to in Sanctuary Wood. It was almost dark by now, and it was quite so after we had had our interview with the captain of the trench we visited. Our talk with him was several times interrupted by heavy machine-gun fire both from his trench and against it, but he told us that it meant nothing, and that this was a very quiet part of the line.

We were all very hungry, but unfortunately this officer could offer us nothing in the way of refreshment, but kept saying that if we had only come a little earlier in the day, he could have regaled us with the choicest of Fortnum and Mason delicacies. These he had given away to his men, he said. I replied that in that case it would be a very sorry substitute for a meal were we to take the will for the deed, and begged that I might be allowed to use his telephone. I then telephoned through to his Brigade Headquarters (no less), and with the utmost assurance requested the brigade-major to order a good supper for twenty officers (*i.e.* the representatives from all our four regiments) at some restaurant in Armentières.

This he promised to do, and after a hasty, but thorough, look at the trenches, we set out to return by the same way as we had come. The communication-trench led for a couple of hundred yards at a time through the houses of one side of the street of a village. This village had previously been the scene of much street fighting, and to clear the houses of the enemy these had been broken into by their side walls all along the street, and the tunnel thus made had subsequently been incorporated in the communication trench to the firing line, and improved here and there with sandbags. The name of this village was Le Touquet. The whole method seemed to me to be dangerous in the extreme, for should the buildings (an easy mark) be brought down by shells, one's communications would be thereby blocked. I afterwards discovered, however, that there was an alternative communication-trench as well.

The supper which we found ready for us at a little restaurant near the now unused railway station was a very merry affair. We did the fullest justice to the fare provided, and drank our fill of excellent red wine. The two bus loads of officers had gradually collected at the inn (whose whereabouts I was never afterwards able definitely to trace), the drivers also were suitably regaled, and at about midnight, very pleased and sleepy, we set out to return to Le Petit Mortier. When we arrived there it was about 2 o'clock in the morning. I looked in on the C.O., and gave him a brief account of the trenches, and then went and sought my blankets on the floor of the *padre's* room, where I slept soundly until 8 o'clock.

CHAPTER 18

Trench Warfare

A dreary morning, (begun at Port Said, 18th December, 1917, and continued at sea) with the rain swishing down upon the decks out of a grey sky. We are loading up with frozen meat and benzine, and sometime this evening we start out for Salonika. The fourth Christmas of the war is but a week ahead, and it will be my third in Macedonia. I am engaged in returning from short leave at home a lengthy and difficult process in these days.

Sixteen months ago, I was also returning from short leave in England, and on that occasion, I wrote a few thousand words of my narrative, bringing it down to the time when I arrived with my regiment at Armentières and took over trenches at Le Touquet, facing the Saxons, who were holding the line in front of a heap of rubble that once was Frelinghein. That was at the end of May, 1915.

A long period of trench warfare was to ensue. My company held the left of the line taken up by the battalion. Two other companies prolonged the line to the right, where some breastworks, untenable by day, extended down to the left bank of the Lys, being occupied at night by a company that was quartered in a deserted farmhouse in rear. Across the river the line was held by two other battalions of our Brigade, in trenches which we were to know very well later on.

Our Battalion Headquarters were in a little house on the northern outskirts of Houplines, close to a lock on the river. To get to them from the trenches one had to walk a long way, down boarded communication-trenches, and through tunnels made in the debris of Le Touquet, until finally one gained the shelter of the railway embankment and emerged into Houplines village.

Our principal occupation in the Le Touquet sector consisted in sniping the enemy trenches, which at one point were only 100 yards distant, and in being sniped at from them. We possessed no preponderance of any sort in those days. Our guns seldom fired, gas was not used, and on the solitary occasion upon which I ordered rifle-grenades to be fired at the enemy trenches the result was not encouraging. The Saxons, I remember, retaliated with rifle-grenades that easily outranged ours, and wounded half a dozen of my men, among them my sergeant-major.

We had not been long in the new part of the line when our brigadier went home on sick leave.

Our C.O. took his place in temporary command of the brigade, and G—— commanded the battalion.

This made me second-in-command, and meant that I was to live at Battalion Headquarters, in Houplines. I remember so well the news coming to me while I was with my company in reserve billets. I had had a welcome night's rest in my little room up the usual steep box-stairs of the poorer type of French village habitation. A mail had arrived from home, and my four subalterns and I were reading our letters and opening parcels of good things. L—— and O—— were of the number, and the latter was loudly denouncing some unknown miscreant who had abstracted the contents of a bottle of Irish whisky from his parcel, and filled the bottle up with water. This sort of trick was not unknown in those days.

Very cheerfully I shouldered my pack that morning, and set out for Headquarters. I had already visited the little house once or twice. It had once been the abode of the manager of a brewery and his family. The brewery faced it across a tiny *place*, which was bounded on one side by the river, and still carried on in a half-hearted sort of way.

"The White House" was a pretty and comfortable little nest. It had had one Boche shell into it, which had only seriously damaged one room, but which had probably been the cause of the family leaving.

There were four large rooms downstairs, one of which we used as an Orderly Room. Of the others, one was the dining-room and one the sitting-room. The fourth had been too much knocked about by the shell to be of any use. Upstairs there were about the same number of bedrooms. G—— occupied the biggest, and in the others were the *padre*, doctor, adjutant, and myself. The quartermaster lived farther back, in Armentières itself, about two miles away. All the rooms were comfortably furnished, and there was a bathroom upstairs. Again, there was a pathetically untidy nursery, and some strong cellars underneath the house, though devoid of wine, were fitted up with chairs and tables as a refuge in case of a bombardment. There were outhouses in which the personnel of Headquarters were housed, and a really beautiful little garden ran down to the river's edge.

In a large kennel attached to the house was a big white *dogue*, very old and helpless. How the people of the house could ever have had the heart to leave him behind we could not think. He speedily became very much attached to us. There were some soldiers' graves in the garden, and a few deep dug-outs. At the far end of the garden was a big, roomy barn, and a farmhouse, still inhabited. The whole place was concealed from the enemy by a fine clump of trees. An abandoned battery position was hidden among the trees.

G—— was not at all well. His wound in the arm had never properly healed, and almost every day our doctor took particles of bone out of it. G——, as was his wont, struggled on gamely, but the work was really too much for him. I took as much of it off his shoulders as I could, and daily did the long journey round the trenches, accompanied by the doctor, and by the C.O.'s orderly, a veteran soldier who cared nothing for shells or bullets, and who would rest and take shelter, or go forward, during a period of "hate" with equal phlegm, according as his C.O. elected to do the one thing or the other. A good deal of enemy shelling did take place at times as one went up to the front trenches, but nearly always the shells went wide.

In the end G—— had to go sick. I think it was on the 2nd June that he handed over to me and went. I was very sorry, for we were old and tried friends.

I was now in command of the battalion, a post which I was to hold for nearly three weeks, after which period G—— returned from his Versailles hospital. I was fortunate in having C—— with me as adjutant, until he, too, went sick, when I was hard put to it to find somebody to replace him.

I shall always look back with pleasure to that time in the White House at Houplines. In spite of the ever-present danger of shells, we managed to be very comfortable and happy.

I had made friends with the lock-keeper. This old man was extraordinarily garrulous. He hated the Boches with a consuming hatred, and used to tell me of how the British skirmishers had driven them before them in those parts earlier in the war, and how drunk the Germans had been as they passed through Armentières, and how interminable their passage had seemed. The British had pressed hard upon their heels, frustrating their attempt to blow up the bridge across the Lys.

The sitting-room of the "White House" was a pleasant place. The weather was very hot, and we spent a good deal of time indoors. We had one of those ingenious little puzzles, very popular at the time at home, called "To Berlin," or something of the sort, in which you had to make a small marble, enclosed in a glass frame, travel along a path beset with pitfalls, until it got safely to its journey's end. We became astonishingly adept at it, and used to time one another over the course. I once actually did it in eleven seconds, the *padre* being next best with seventeen.

Unfortunately, the battalion suffered several losses from sniping and shelling during the period in which I held the command, and somehow these things always seemed doubly distressing when they occurred in a "quiet" portion of the line. I remember particularly the death of the officer who had taken over the command of my company from me, and who had formed one of our party coming out from home; also, that of a sergeant whose acquaintance I had made in the course of my rounds only a few hours before his death. The officer was shot through the head as he was firing over the parapet of his trench, exasperated at the persistence of an enemy sniper opposite. The sergeant was in command of a small post, guarding an important bridge, and I had been much struck, when I went round, by his replies to my questions and by the general resourcefulness which he had evinced.

I had asked the adjutant, when we had passed on, to tell me something about him, and it had appeared that he was a well-educated man, speaking French fluently, and possessing a good knowledge of the classics. He was what is known in Ireland as a "spoiled priest," that is, he had studied for the Church and then given it up. On the outbreak of war, he, with so many thousands of young Irishmen, had joined the army, believing firmly in the justice of England's cause. He had risen rapidly to his present rank, and was looked up to by all his men.

Shortly after dark that night a company had to go out to repair some breastworks in the low-lying ground by the Lys, and a sniper's bullet, fired at random, killed the poor "spoiled priest." We buried him in the little cemetery on the way up to Le Ruage Château—a big house at the entrance to the communication-trenches on the right bank of the river. The body was sewn up in a greatcoat. There was no Union Jack available with which to cover it, but I bethought me of a large French flag that I had found in an upper room of our Headquarters, where it had been laid by to be used for gala days. We covered the body with this.

In one part of Houplines there was a town hall, with a high belfry, which the gunners used to use as an observation-station. One day the Germans decided that they would have it down, and they opened fire on it. The shells burst in the little place just outside our Headquarters, and I gave orders for everybody to take to the cellars and dug-outs. It was very dark in the cellars, and every time a shell burst outside the concussion blew out all our candles. When we emerged into the open on the cessation of the bombardment the belfry was gone.

I had noticed when we took over the trenches on the right bank of the river that our Engineers were carrying out mining operations, and for the 18th June (Waterloo Day) a surprise was being prepared for the Boche. This was to take the form of the explosion, first of a *camouflet*, then of a mine, followed by a few minutes' bombardment of the crater. A *camouflet* is a sort of subdued mine, which just suffices to shake the earth in on top of any of the enemy who may themselves be mining in the vicinity. That they were doing so we knew, for only a few days before they had exploded a small mine just short of portion of our parapet.

Punctually at the time arranged the *camouflet* went off, and the other things duly followed. That night the bodies of two Saxons were recovered from the scene of the explosion. One was that of a very tall man, fair and handsome; the other was a quite young soldier almost a boy. Both had been smothered. The younger had a handkerchief tied over his mouth and nostrils. It must have been tied there by his friend, for it bore the older man's initials. My men gave them decent burial behind the trench, and planted a cross over the grave, whereupon was written:

Here lie two Saxon soldiers, who died bravely. R.I.P.

About this time C——, the adjutant, went sick. He had been very bad for some time, but would not leave his work. He was bent double with pain. In the end I had to force him to go, and to lift him into the ambulance. For some days I had to run the battalion with an inexperienced youngster as adjutant. But he did his best, and things went quite well. And then G—— came back, and I became second-in-command again. After a few more days L—— arrived from home. He was senior to us both. I went back to the trenches to command my old company.

For nearly three months from that time I commanded "C" Company in the trenches east and south-east of Armentières. On the whole it was a quiet time, though almost every day brought a few casualties in its train. About every four or five days we came out for a brief rest. The men were quartered in a large factory, while the officers were billeted on families of the working-class, in tiny but scrupulously clean rooms. Every now and then the enemy would shell the billets, whereupon the men would run out into dug-outs, and the inhabitants would take to their cellars. My company mess was in a brick house at the end of a row, and in it we had many a cheery meal. The worst trial was the flies, which swarmed over everything. Outside the house was a strawberry patch in a delightful little wood, through which ran a line of disused trenches.

In August the battalion was moved back along the Armentières-Estaires road to a hamlet known as Fort Rompu, where it rested for a few days. We then moved down a little further to the south of Armentières, and took over other trenches near Gris Pot and Fleurbaix. When in Battalion Reserve my Company Headquarters were situated in a pleasant farm, which had been christened by English soldiers earlier in the war "Streaky Bacon Farm," from its being built of alternate red and white courses of brick. The buildings, with their picturesque, high-pitched red roofs, were grouped around a paved courtyard, in the middle of which was the inevitable midden. The dwelling-house occupied one side, and the others were formed by huge barns and stables, not unlike those one sees in Sussex.

Just outside the gate of the farm was a stone horse-pond, into which the great farmhorses were sent, two and two, every morning before beginning the day's work, and again on returning in the evening. They were driven, with much shouting and cracking of whips, down a steep incline between walls; and at the bottom, which was so formed as to oblige them to turn round one way and come out again, the water just reached their flanks. The whole process of ablution was most picturesque, and the huge beasts seemed to enjoy it thoroughly.

When not on duty these farm-horses used to graze in the fields close to the house. The fields were pitted with shell-craters, and the owner of the house told me that he had already lost two horses from shell-fire. There was a dear old grey mare grazing close to where we stood, and with regard to her he told me a remarkable story.

It appeared that when the Germans fell back through Armentières earlier in the war they commandeered all the horses they could lay hands on, including this grey mare. They took her away towards Lille; but one night, about a week afterwards, the old man who looked after the stables heard something butting at the gate. He went out, and there was the mare, covered from head to foot with mud, and terribly exhausted. She must have found her way back over miles of unfamiliar country, and how she had avoided recapture on those crowded roads remained a mystery. While we were in this billet the people received news that a brother of theirs was lying dangerously wounded in a hospital in Amiens, and the old mother posted off at once to be with him; but they told me afterwards that she had arrived only in time to see him *dans son cercueil*. (In his coffin.)

Trench life never bored me, as it did some people. There was always enough incident to prevent that. (Of course, I was extremely fortunate in being spared the awful 1914-15 winter!) The day used to begin with "Stand to!" one hour or so before dawn. Whichever officer kept the last watch of the night would awaken the others. The N.C.O.'s would rouse the men whose turn it had been to sleep on the fire-step; and in the weird semi-darkness and cold a line of muffled figures, with fixed bayonets, would stand peering over the parapet into No Man's Land, while the company commander walked along all the fire-bays, and each platoon commander accompanied him down his particular portion of the trench. Then, when the light was fully come, the company commander would pass the word along to "Stand down!" and the ordinary routine of the day would begin.

One's soldier servant had meanwhile been preparing a cup of hot *café au lait* at the mess kitchen (generally situated in a close support-trench, or in a communication-trench), and the little band of officers of the company would gather there to drink it. How good it was! One of my subalterns had managed to procure a terrier, and after our *café au lait* we used to go and hunt the droves of enormous rats that infested the trenches. It was a very game little dog, and must have killed pretty nearly its weight in rats every day.

Often, of course, all the officers had to stay up at night. The days, compared to the nights, were always quiet. But at night working-parties and patrols had to go out, rations to be brought up, and a dozen other things done. How different from what I had pictured, judging by my experiences in October! Then my only rest (when I got any) had been at night. The days had been very busy, and that, too, when they were short. I used to wonder what would happen with the long days and short nights of summer. Trench warfare had indeed wrought changes!

I had a first-rate pony now, called "Tommy," a polo pony that had belonged to the regiment in India; and when we were out of the trenches I used to go for many long rides behind the line. On one occasion I went as far as Merville, where I met some of the 15th

Sikhs, a regiment which I had known in India. But our most usual excursion used to be into Armentières, where there were some very good shops, and where one could get a good dinner and a bottle of wine. The town possessed no striking buildings. The church was well proportioned, but modern. The streets were broad and well shaded. The inhabitants displayed the greatest *sang froid* in face of almost daily shelling, and it was a common thing to hear of civilians being killed by shells in the market-square.

No great bombardment took place, however, while we knew the town, though there were always plenty of rumours that one was about to do so. But only the other day I heard that the whole place had been destroyed by a most savage bombardment, and 1,500 of the inhabitants suffocated by gas shells. I only hope it is not true.

West of Armentières there was a village called Erquinghem-sur-la Lys, which possessed a very beautiful twelfth-century church. I often used to visit it on my way from the town to our billets at Fort Rompu. It was so cool, so simple, so symmetrical, and yet strong; so austere, and yet it seemed to glow internally. Its deeply-recessed altar to Joan of Arc was always a blaze of candles and adorned with tricolours. It had a beautiful tower, of the type that recurs throughout that part of France—wide for its height, and coming quickly to a point; and it had a wonderful peal of bells.

The groups of ancient farms that studded the country were very picturesque. They bore suggestive names—Froid Nid, Fleur d'Écosse, Finde-la-Guerre (which peace or longing for peace did this commemorate, I wonder?), La Rolanderie—these were some of them. And then the inns—*Au Rendezvous des Pêcheurs*—*Pécheurs* our *padre* said it should have been, for he was a stickler for veracity—*Au Point du Jour, Au Gazon Vert*, etc., etc. For great part of August, I was employed, whenever we were out of the trenches, in building a "strong point" at Bois Grenier. I used to work on this all day with a large party, and in the evening, I would ride back to Fort Rompu through the teeming cornfields, in the moonlight. The harvest had grown and ripened, in the care of those devoted women of France, within easy shelling distance of the line.

We made one more minor move before I got my leave—to a suburb called Chapelle d'Armentières, where we occupied trenches at Ferme du Biez. I obtained ten days' leave from there, after I had been for four months continuously at the Front.

How well I remember the feeling of joyful anticipation as I buckled on my pack and equipment, and set off down the long communi-cation-trench! At one point in it a sentry stopped me, and asked me where I was going. "A long way—to Tipperary," I said, and ran. When I emerged from the trenches into the street (it was the same street down which the motor-bus had brought us in error when I first came to look at the Armentières trenches) I had a considerable distance to walk before I could get to Brigade Headquarters and my pony. That particular bit of road used to be shelled almost daily. I walked very fast.

I found my pony and groom waiting for me, and on that lovely Sunday morning of early September we set off together to ride to railhead, which was then at Steenwerck, about two hours' journey from where we started.

I travelled down to Boulogne with some old friends, one of whom I had known at Stonyhurst many years before. He was full of secrecy concerning a new and deadly gas which he declared he knew for a fact we had just invented. But, then, everybody one met was always the retailer of the most astounding stories concerning gas.

My leave was—as I need hardly say—extremely pleasant; also, it went like a flash. The greater part of it I spent in my Tipperary home. (I had not deceived the sentry!)

CHAPTER 19

In the Somme Trenches

On returning from leave I found the battalion concentrated just behind the line, at Chapelle d'Armentières, and under orders to move down to the Somme. About the 28th September we set off to march to Hazebrouck. We marched great part of the day and night. The men were in fine form, and some of the companies carried huge Belgian and French flags, which they had obtained no one knew how. It was a tiring march, and I let my subalterns take turns at riding my pony, while I did my share of walking. After many hours we turned into a large field some way short of Hazebrouck. It was very dark, and I think it had begun to rain. The men slept where they halted, while the officers took possession of a farmhouse, where there was some food to be had and straw to sleep on.

After seeing that my men had something to eat and were as comfortable as the circumstances would permit, I left my subalterns and those of the other companies to have a meal together in the large living-room of the farm, while I repaired to Battalion Headquarters, which had been established in a better house further up the road, and where I knew a cheery welcome awaited me. When I returned, an hour or two later, to the farm, I found that my subalterns had secured some wine and done themselves pretty well. As I passed the windows, I caught the words, "Let's pull the ladder up and pretend we're all asleep!"

"Oho, my boys!" said I to myself, "two can play at that game." And without disturbing the revellers I went quickly up the ladder by which we gained access to our loft, and pulled it up after me.

Presently my youngsters, fully believing that I was still away at dinner, came boisterously across the stable-yard to where the ladder should have been. Then there were astonished exclamations, followed by much groping and searching. It was a long time before the first head appeared at the window of the barn, and to this day I do not know how they all got up. One of them switched on a pocket-lamp, and the first thing it disclosed to their astonished gaze was the ladder. The second was me. They simply subsided where they stood, without looking for their blankets, and in the morning, I made them fix the ladder in position while I majestically descended to perform my ablutions at the pump.

We spent a day or two at Hazebrouck, and were reviewed by General P——. We were leaving one corps to go to another, and he had come to bid us goodbye. Company commanders had to be mounted for the occasion, and I remember how amused we were at the antics of one officer who was not very much at home on the back of a horse, and who got in the way of the general's motor on the road, and could not induce his steed to move either forward or back. The general told us in his farewell speech that we were going down to the Somme to stiffen up some of the divisions of the New Army, and to take over part of the line from the French. He congratulated us on our fine appearance.

Some officers had to be sent on in advance to look at the new trenches, and, to my great delight, G—— and I went together. We travelled down in a closed wagon, with plenty of straw in it, through St. Pol, Doullens, and Amiens. It was a leisurely business, and we had plenty of time to admire the scenery. That is the best way to see the country—from a troop-train. The pace is always slow and there are many stops, both authorised and unauthorised, *en route*.

I think it was at a little place called Guilleaucourt that we arrived at last, and there we had to wait for several hours of the night before the motor-bus came to take us on to Mericourt.

We tried to obtain some coffee at an inn, but the uncouth proprietor of the place absolutely refused to serve us. I must say he was an exception to the usual run of innkeepers one met. I shall always remember the fine sarcasm with which our French officer interpreter thanked him for his hospitality to strangers when, at last, we left the house. We were all of us dog-tired when we reached Mericourt, and as there was nowhere for us to billet at that hour, we crept into some barns and slept amid the straw. Only for two hours, however, and on a Sunday morning we all trooped out of the village, with our Interpreter as guide, to walk across the rolling downs to the village of Cappy, in which were the Headquarters of the French Brigade which

154

we were about to relieve.

It was a glorious autumn morning. The scenery was quite different from anything we had had experience of lately, and the wide views which one got along and across the valley of the Somme were well calculated to brace and cheer one. We had to cross a high ridge, from which we looked in one direction towards the German country and Peronne, and in the other towards Amiens, with the fine towers of Corby showing up in the middle distance and scattered villages with beautiful names on every hand. Our guide knew them all and pointed them out to us. Then we swung down the hill (avoiding a portion of the road which was marked "Dangerous by day. Exposed to enemy fire"), and after marching along the Cappy Canal for some miles we arrived at the village of that name, and had breakfast of eggs and coffee at an inn.

We had an hour or so to wait before our guides were ready to take us to the trenches. I went to look at the beautiful little church, in the open space in front of which a company of French infantry was "falling in" under its officers, ready to march off to the trenches. It moved off as I waited, very smart and business-like. I noticed that the reliefs in these parts were carried out by day. (We soon adopted this practice, so opposed to that to which we had hitherto been accustomed).

To get to the trenches we had to walk a good way out of Cappy uphill, and then, for a distance which seemed interminable, through deep communication-trenches, up to Battalion Headquarters. Our trenches were called the "*Secteur de Dompierre.*" They were opposite a demolished village of that name, through which the German line ran. Four adjoining trenches were to be allotted to our Battalion, called respectively "*Sucrerie*," "*Peupliers*," "*Galeries*," and "*Gobelins*," the latter in playful allusion to the manner in which the officers' *cagnas* (French slang for dug-outs) had been hung with tapestries composed of sacking, to keep away the damp.

"*Galeries*" was so named from the fact of its having many mine shafts and tunnels driven underneath it. This was to be my trench. It was the most dangerous of the lot, as I shall later on relate.

None of the trenches were strong according to our ideas. They had very little parapet or parados, being sunk almost to ground-level, and such as there was, was only in very few cases bullet-proof. Considerable portions of the trenches were not even held, but had been strongly wired overhead, while machine-gun emplacements had been made at either end of such portions so as to sweep them with their fire. Not at all a bad arrangement. The dug-outs were far superior to anything we had ever experienced.

My first adventure in connection with these trenches was a very amusing one. We all (that is to say, our five officers and their three or four) had been round the lines, and had closely inspected everything (except the *feuillees*—our attempts to inspect these were successfully baffled), and the company commander had given us a slap-up lunch in his *cagna*. He was a charming fellow, a Gascon named A——, of the 414th Infantry. We did ourselves so well that before very long we had reached the stage of calling one another *Mon vieux*. This I presently bettered, to his huge delight and that of his subalterns, by calling him *Tartarin*.

After lunch we all had to pose for our portraits—a real *entente* scene—and then my newly-made friend said he would take us round his trenches again and show us a thing or two.

All along the trench at intervals of a few yards were recesses cut in the parapet, and in each of these was a bomb, which only needed the setting of a certain adjunct for it to be at "danger." After that, in four seconds, it would explode. My friend, as he passed along the trench, would light-heartedly seize a bomb and proceed to demonstrate its action. He would set it going, and then wave it gracefully round his head for about three seconds, before tossing it over the parapet, where it would explode with a terrific bang. Sometimes he would throw one in the wrong direction over the parados. All the time he would be talking to me in the true Gascon style.

I began to think this rather a poor game—especially as I noticed out of the corner of my eye that all my other friends, both French and British, had quietly withdrawn. But I felt sure that the *capitaine* was gasconading, that he knew very well what he was doing, and that he was only trying to pull my leg. So, I said that it appeared very easy, but that the French bombs were quite different from ours—and might I try one? That settled him, and we proceeded afterwards in a more normal manner.

When we got back to Cappy we obtained a lift in a French car in the direction of Mericourt, whence we had come that morning, and after going a, few miles we fell in with the battalion, which was marching up. We halted near Froissy Wood, and everybody had a meal and a rest. A heavy cannonade had broken out in the direction of the trenches. We moved off for these as evening was coming on. The move into a new section of trenches is always fraught with uncertainty and anxiety; but the men were in good form.

Our first taking over from the French was well managed and expeditiously done. The officer whom I relieved very kindly remained in with me even after his own men had marched out an instance of real friendliness and *camaraderie*, which I shall always remember. I think our men were a bit puzzled during the transfer, but they hit it off very well with the French. The attitude used always to be one of mutual amused admiration. As befitting the senior company commander, I was told off to hold the "*Galeries*" trench. It was a weird place, honeycombed with underground passages.

The first day after we had taken over a message arrived from the French commander (under whom for the time we were) to the effect that the Germans seemed about to explode a mine under my trench, and that *le danger peut être immédiat*. French engineers had been left behind to listen in the mine shafts, and they had reported that the "tapping," which had been going on for some time beneath them, had ceased. This, it appeared, usually meant business.

The French engineers immediately began to sink yet another counter-mine, but there was little chance of its being in time. My orders, which were in French, were to the effect that a certain portion of my trench—where the *fourneau* (furnace) of the mine had been located—was to be evacuated forthwith, and a retrenchment dug in rear so as to block the evacuated portion. It was expected that the moment the enemy exploded his mine his infantry would dash forward, under cover of a barrage, to occupy the crater. This I was to prevent by hurrying my own men forward from the retrenchment into the same crater, where a brisk piece of business with bomb and bayonet was expected to occur. The battalion bombers were lent me for the occasion, and I disposed them on the flanks of the evacuated portion.

I lost no time in withdrawing my men, and as soon as darkness came on, I set to work, with the aid of our engineers, to start digging the retrenchment. We had to work in a chalk soil, difficult to dig, difficult to revet, and almost impossible to conceal. When day broke, we had got through an extraordinary amount of work, but the retrenchment was scarcely fightable yet. One of the French *Postes d'Écoute* reported that tapping had begun again down under our feet. I went into the shaft and listened for myself. I put the antennae of an overgrown stethoscope to my ears, and there sure enough was the *tap, tap, tap* going on below me. Every now and then I could also hear the sound of some sort of a truck or trolley being rolled along, as if to cart the excavated earth away from the shaft.

It was most uncanny. However, as long as the tapping went on the danger could hardly be "immediate," and it went on for another day and night, during which time we worked like slaves on our retrenchment. That night the enemy sent up more flares than usual, but we could not afford to stop work. Marvellous to relate, though, he did not shell us. In that he made a great mistake. A company of the 2nd D. C.L.I, was sent up to strengthen me, and I was glad to have its help. Its officers and mine shared a dug-out for mess. I took a couple of young subalterns, who were game for a lark, out with me into a disused listening-post in front of our trench, quite close to the Boche lines, and from it I fired an enormous rocket straight at the top of their parapet. It went off with a tremendous hiss and blaze, and must have made them jump. We climbed back into our trench, shaking with laughter.

The truth was that one had to do something amusing, in order to relieve the tension. Living over a mine is very wearing work, and I should not like to have to do it again. Hitherto the good old earth has always been your best friend, and now even it is in league against you.

In the morning the "tapping" had ceased. But by now our retrenchment was fairly well completed, and we could await events with the imperturbability conferred by the taking of every practical measure of safety. Of course, the evacuated portion of trench had to be patrolled from time to time. Picked men were told off to do this, and I used to give it my personal attention, too.

At about 5 o'clock in the evening I was walking through the evacuated portion, and had just reached the point that had been pointed out to me by the French engineers as the probable *fourneau*, when I saw a light shining from a disused dug-out just over the spot. Smoke was issuing from it, too. I went into the dug-out, and was horrified to see a figure in a khaki greatcoat bending over a fire on the floor. I had issued very strict orders that nobody, except officers and patrols, was to enter the evacuated bit of trench. I called angrily to the man. He looked round, and I saw that it was B——, a slow-witted, rather queer old man of my company. He was making himself some tea! He was a man who liked to be by himself, and seeing this quiet bit of trench, with a nice empty dug-out in it, and plenty of pieces of wood lying about, he had judged it an excellent place for an undisturbed meal.

War is, perhaps, at its cruellest for the young country recruit, and for men of this sort, who come from some quiet Irish countryside. Poison gas, explosive bullets, intensive bombardments, tetanus—for men like these! At its cruellest, I would say, when it has struck them down. Until then I do not think they take a thousandth part of it in. Once it has maimed them or poisoned them, however, one feels guilty by reason of one's superior education. It is like being detected in some base conspiracy by somebody who depends on one.

But I had men, too, from the Irish countryside who, knowing all that there was to know about war's horrors, yet eagerly and disdainfully encountered them. Such a one was a man whom I had in my company, and who when out of the trenches was the most troublesome and incorrigible man I had. But in the trenches, he became transformed. I remember once, when heavy shelling had driven nearly everybody underground, finding him standing on the fire-step, calmly looking over the parapet, while he smoked his pipe.

He was a man who always erected a tiny altar in a recess cut in the fire-bay, and placed on it a picture of Our Lady which he had found in some ruined cottage. He was standing close to it now, and he had lighted two tiny wax candles on either side of the picture. This was a man for whom, later on, I strained every nerve to obtain a few days' leave when leave was officially closed. He had begged me to let him go home to see "me little sister, Sir, she's dying," I couldn't get the leave for him, alas! and the sister died.

G—— came up to see me during the time of greatest tension, and when he was going back to his post at Battalion Headquarters, I went part of the way with him, to see him to the confines of my dominion. We thought we should save time at one point by taking a short cut underground, through one of the long galleries which the French had constructed for this purpose. He was rather doubtful as to the wisdom of this course, but I thought I knew the way thoroughly, and induced him to attempt it. Unfortunately, there were several ramifications and branches to the main tunnel, and into one of these we must have strayed, for we walked for a long and eerie way in the pitch darkness without coming to daylight. To make things a hundred times worse a bombardment started overhead. We could feel, rather than hear, the bursting of the shells.

Heavens! I thought, the mine is about to be touched off, and here are we, like rats in a hole. My company might at any moment now be plunged into a desperate encounter, and its leader away! Besides that, if it were a big mine, it would be certain to act, too, as a *camouflet*, and shake the earth in on us. We turned and ran back, and fortunately we took all the right turnings this time. We emerged into the open once more. I made for my *Poste de Commandement,* and G—— hurried off, via the communication-trench this time, to Battalion Headquarters. The bombardment had died down, and the mine had not gone up. Hastily I made a tour of my trench. All was in order, and everything ready according to the plans which I had made. My understudy was where I had placed him when I went off with G——.

CHAPTER 20

For This Relief Much Thanks

The mine did not go up that night or any of the succeeding days or nights until I was relieved. The strain of living over such a volcano was very great, though, and I longed for the time of my deliverance. I did not get much sleep during all that time—I think I was eight days and nights over the mine. My dug-out was a very deep one, down a steep flight of steps. It was simply swarming with enormous rats, who looked upon man as an intruder, and would scarcely make room for him at all. When I went into that dug-out and struck a match, a sort of black drop-scene would ascend the walls. It was rats climbing up behind the brushwood lining of the dug-out. We killed hundreds of the brutes. M—— of the D. C.L.I, made a sort of lance, with a long pole and knife, and sat up all one night, when he was on duty, dispatching the rats that ran across the doorway of the dug-out.

Sometimes one would meet a dozen of the creatures in a narrow trench, as they lolloped along, clumsy with gorging on recently-buried dead. One used to kick them along the trench like sodden footballs. Often, as I sat by night in some part of my long trench-line, I would see a string of rats moving along the top of the parapet or parados against the sky. Their evil heads were down, and one saw nothing but their rounded backs, making them look like a row of skulls—the dead arisen from beneath the trenches for a veritable dance of death. It was an orgy of rats.

Yes, the nights in those trenches were horrible, and we preferred the days. You had the blessed sunshine then, and although the appearance of calm was deceptive, it was impossible not to take pleasure in the singing of the larks, and in the vivid poppies that nodded bravely along the edges of the communication-trenches.

I used to spend a good deal of time in a carefully concealed "sniper's post," practising my marksmanship on points where I imagined enemy snipers to be hidden. We had some very efficient sharpshooters in the company, and we soon established a superiority in this respect over the enemy. Then, about that time, *The Times* brought out a splendid series of "broadsheets" for trench reading, reproducing passages from great authors. My people sent me all of them, and they proved an inestimable boon.

One day I went down one of our mine shafts. It was brilliantly lighted by electric light, but there was not a soul in it. How far it extended I do not know. It was supposed to lead under one German sap and over another. At the bottom of it I turned, and came up by another shaft which joined it. It was good to be in the daylight again.

But at last the night of my relief came. My company had had all the hard work and all the anxiety, and we were tired out. The other companies had had a comparatively easy time. In the "*Sucrerie*" trench alone they had had some casualties, but this was owing to men venturing out to collect pieces of coal from a huge heap that was lying in front of the abandoned sugar refinery. There was a large graveyard in this sector, which had been shelled to pieces, and its great crucifix, though still erect, had been riddled with bullets.

We were relieved by a battalion of our own brigade, and they in their turn, after three or four days, were succeeded by a battalion of another brigade. We heard afterwards that the mine had gone up during the latter's tour of duty. A big figure was named for the casualties. Probably it was much exaggerated. I trust it was. But the uncertainty was typical of things in wartime. One knows nothing definite concerning other battalions in one's own brigade, nothing beyond the vaguest rumours about other brigades, while as to other divisions, they scarcely seem to exist, and a danger, which in one's own case has been a matter of deep and acute anxiety, ceases, on being transferred to the shoulders of strangers, to have anything much more than an academic interest for one.

My company was about the last to complete the relief that night, but I took them across country in the dark, thereby saving several weary miles, and bringing them in in great good humour long before the others. When we arrived our Company Q.M.S. had our billets ready, and was waiting for us. We got the best billets, a good meal, and a sound sleep. My subalterns and I were lodged in a clean little house. I had a good room to myself, and for ten hours I slept the sleep of the just.

I liked at once the country in which we were billeted. The little villages were charming. This one, Chuignolles, was merely a hamlet of a single street, and not unlike an Irish village, though cleaner and more picturesque. Its church had a pathetic, shrapnel-riddled spire, so twisted that it looked like an inverted parsnip. Chuignes was the next village to it, in the direction of the trenches, and in the other direction was Proyart, standing on high ground and containing a beautiful church; and Mericourt, away across the downs, lay in the direction of the Somme.

The room which I occupied in my billet had evidently belonged to the son of the house, now away fighting on the borders of Alsace. On the mantelpiece were photographs of him and his *poilu* friends, and above it there hung a large framed diploma of membership of a rifle-club, bearing the apt motto—*vis tel que tu vises—droit!*

The walls were adorned with quaint old pictures of the Saints, painted in crude colours upon glass. I tried to buy some of these from the lady of the house, but the only one with which she would part was that of St. Peter, and this I caused to be carefully packed by the Pioneer-Sergeant and sent home. It was a very curious picture, with the cock crowing right into the old man's face. It would be interesting to know something more about those paintings on glass. I came across other specimens (all dealing with religious subjects) in different houses in that part of France.

Early in our stay at Chuignolles I heard that "my general" of the galloper days had been killed. It was a great blow. He had just been given command of our corps, and I had been looking forward keenly to a renewal of our friendship.

The most beautiful little town in the neighbourhood of our village was Bray-sur-Somme. I rode over there one Sunday afternoon in company with our *padre*, and we visited its fine Transition church. Afterwards we cracked a bottle of wine with a noted Falstaffian innkeeper of the place. He knew all about the war, and drew me a map to illustrate some good news that had come in from another portion of the Front (Champagne, I think) that morning. He was a great Freethinker, and polite to the *padre* strictly on his merits. After that we went out into the Grande Place to listen to a British divisional band playing. Nothing could have been more peaceful. We had not yet broken the sort of tacit agreement come to between the French and Germans, whereby neither side shelled villages behind the lines.

But, of course, this town, like all French towns, had cruelly felt the strain of war. Not a family but had had its loss. There were no young men left at all—only children and old people. It was pathetic to see a few old members of a brass band, that had once been the pride of the town, creeping out into the autumn sunshine to listen to the strains. I talked to one of them, and that was how I knew who the old fellows were.

How little the people of England realise even now what it means for a *whole country* to be at war! The Mayor of Chuignolles used to describe to me how, when the Germans had swept through the place, on their retreat from the Marne, only he and a few other old men were left to bury the many hundreds of dead that lay about the fields. At first the young boys had been called upon to help, but this had been discontinued. I remember seeing a big grave between Chuignolles and Mericourt in which forty Germans had been buried. The first rough inscription put up had talked of *Quarante Boches*; but later this had been replaced by a decent cross, and the word *Allemands* substituted for "Boches."

I used often while at Chuignolles to go up the street to have lunch or dinner at Battalion Headquarters. Those were very enjoyable meals, and we always had a bottle or two of the best wine procurable in the neighbourhood. And here let me state that the military wallets, or holsters, far from being the encumbrance on the forepart of a saddle that some foolish people would maintain, are exactly large enough to take a bottle each of wine!

The woman who owned the house in which the mess was quartered was of the scolding type of French housewife—an unpleasant sort of person to live with, but no doubt compelled by stern necessity to pinch and pare, and possessed of admirable qualities. Still, it was unpleasant to find her counting the knives and forks and plates every time we had had a meal, and looking through the few wretched books that the room possessed to see whether we had torn out any of the pages. In fact, she became a confounded nuisance after a bit. But one fine day our soldier-cook left a leg of mutton exposed in the larder, the dog of the house took it, and when we recovered it from him it was only fit for the incinerator.

Such a calamity would have kept a French household talking for a year, and this hard-faced woman felt the blow acutely, even if vicariously. It so outraged the eternal *comme-il-faut*. It gave me my opportunity, though. I finished up by calling her *malheureuse*, (miserable). *Vous êtes malheureuse. Madame*, I declared. She didn't like that at all. Ever

164

afterwards she trusted us with the knives and forks.

Our next tour of duty was in slightly different trenches, and on coming out into rest we were billeted in a damp village on the left bank of the Somme, named Morcourt. It was here, early in October, that I got the news of poor Ninian Crichton-Stuart's death at Loos. The constant loss of friends is the hardest thing to bear in this war.

While we were at Morcourt we practised a new method of attack, in which the men had to fire from the shoulder while advancing. I do not think it had much of a vogue. I also got a friend to take me into Amiens in his motor, and visited its superb cathedral.

Next to Morcourt, farther downstream, there was a pretty village named Cherisy, with an ancient church, and to get to it you could ride either by the road that led along the river bank, or by one that scaled some high ground behind Morcourt and passed close to the edge of a steep cliff. On this cliff one day I met an old man who described to me how some French soldiers had killed one of an *Uhlan* patrol across the river, from that very spot, in 1870. I used to offer a prize for the first man of my company to climb up or down this cliff when we were out at exercise. What a scramble used to ensue! We officers were always first, and then a string of men would come in—the latter wildly striving for a pint of beer.

My great amusement in this part of the country, when out of the trenches, consisted in riding long distances to visit little towns and villages, and in this way I visited about a dozen places and got to know the country very well.

Another set of trenches that we held on the Somme were further to the south of Dompierre. To get to them we had to march through Raincourt and Framerville to a totally destroyed village called Herleville. I think we billeted in the first-named place for a while, and then at Framerville, whither we used to come to rest. Here we were kept a considerable time in reserve in order that we might instruct the officers of a Kitchener division, who were in need of tuition. They were apt pupils, but needed tactful handling. Instruction had to be imparted in this sort of way:—

This morning we shall talk about 'listening posts.' Now I don't know what you fellows have found to be best with regard to these (they had been in the trenches for a few hours), but we have always found, etc., etc., etc.

It succeeded admirably, and we were great friends. It was said, however, that a neighbouring unit was not so successful, simply because it could not forget that it was a Regular unit of the Old Army, or make allowances for the newness of these officers who had been attached to it for instruction.

In Raincourt there were still German billeting inscriptions remaining on the doors of the houses. That on mine was to the effect that the people in this particular house were "good." I was mindful of this when the ancient *beldame* upon whom I was billeted asked me to write down my name and regiment for her. I was taking no chances.

Some heavy shelling took place while we were in the Herleville trenches, principally, be it noted, by our guns. This was the *first time* in my experience that our artillery was permitted to give more than it got. England had only just begun to learn its lesson. What a joy it was to all of us to hear those British shells going over! It must, however, be admitted that a fairly high proportion of them were "duds." Our men had read a lot about the Society ladies who had devoted themselves to the making of munitions (or whose portraits in the papers said they had), and whenever a shell failed to burst you would hear them say to one another, quite casually, "There goes a Duchess!"

One fine morning we had just gone into these trenches for about the fourth time when with incredible rapidity the news spread that we were to be relieved by the French, and to concentrate behind the line. Many were the rumours as to what was to happen to us. The Serbian crisis was in full swing, and the consensus of opinion was that we were to be sent to "Serbia."

In due course the French took over from us. The officer who relieved me had been a commercial traveller in the United States before the war; but he knew his job. His men were a seasoned-looking lot of veterans. With the extraordinary *insouciance* of their nation they swarmed out over the parapet, as soon as they had arrived in the trench, to look at the wire! Wonderful to relate, the enemy did not fire on them. But they could scarcely have better advertised the fact that there had been an international relief. The French captain remarked on the youthful appearance of my men, adding, however, that they were admirably turned out. Certainly, the difference in age between his men and mine was very striking.

My experience of the French was that they ruled their men almost entirely by sentiment, and not with a hard-and-fast discipline. And their men seemed to respond admirably to it. They often disregarded non-essentials (which with us would have been reckoned very nearly essentials), but they were perfectly cognisant of the things that really mattered, and performed them as a matter of course. Thus, with us it would be looked upon as in the last degree unpardonable if a battalion commander did not go round his trenches very frequently, especially when there was "nothing doing."

A French commanding officer, on the contrary, need not even see his trenches, except in case of imminent danger. But he would feel perfectly confident that when the time came for him to put himself at the head of his men (as he enthusiastically would) to lead or repel an attack, everything would be correct in every detail. We are rigid, the French are flexible; we are unimaginative, the French highly-strung and nervous; our officers and men fight well because cowardice and yielding are looked down upon; the French do so because among them bravery and glory are idealised. And with us patriotism is only to be inferred from what we do; whereas with the French it is first of all loudly proclaimed, and then steadfastly and unwaveringly followed.

We may take the first point, for it is typical of much—the difference between our rigidity and their flexibility. If our men were seen coming streaming back from a position, almost helter-skelter, their heads down, their shoulders up, anybody would know that the position had been lost. If the French did it every one would feel quite confident that they would be racing back again within the hour, heads up and eyes mystically shining. And, whereas we had stood still all through, they would be farther forward in the end than when they had started.

Then, it is scarcely conceivable that any troops but the English would be guilty of such banality as is to be seen in the nomenclature of any set of English trenches in any part of the line. There must be a "Piccadilly Circus," there must be a "Dover Street," an "Albemarle Street," "Clarges Street," "Down Street," and all the rest of the pointless tomfoolery. It might be comprehensible if the troops were always London troops. The French generally named their trenches after the officers who had constructed them, or after salient features in the neighbourhood. They could never have descended to a "Love Lane," which was the one variant from the London street business that never failed to appear in English trenches.

CHAPTER 21

To Some Other Theatre of War

After the relief was completed, we marched away down the main Amiens road, and for the first night we halted at Lamotte-en-Santerre. The men were in good form, but they were trying to carry far too many things, and when we left this place the next day much stuff had to be "dumped." That day's march was to have far-reaching consequences for me, although I little realised it at the time, for that night, on reaching our billets, I was specially complimented by the C.O., at the brigadier's instigation, on the turn-out and marching of my company. I thought no more of it at the time, but it was to make me a brigade-major later on.

Our doubts as to our destination had been set at rest that day. A fine band had played us through Villers-Bretonneux, each company in turn, and the colonel of the battalion to which the band belonged had told me that the 22nd Division had already gone. We went into camp (a rare occurrence) that night, on some high ground to the south of Boves, and after the men had been fed and made comfortable a cheery party of officers met me at an inn in the little town and enjoyed a late, but excellent, dinner.

From Boves we marched the next day to Pissy, where my company was billeted in a large house that had seen better days. Here we entertained the C.O. and battalion staff to dinner, and also gave the platoon sergeants a banquet, in which turkey formed the staple diet. The people of the house—farmers of a fairly well-to-do class—dined with the sergeants. What a picture they would have made—the big, cheerful kitchen-living-room, the *patron* and his wife, the veteran Irish N.C.O.'s, and the sergeant-major carving the turkey, and gallantly pressing an enormous helping upon the astonished and amused *Madame!*

I looked in upon this party once during the evening, because I wanted to wish my N.C.O.'s good-luck, and also to see that a certain one among them was enjoying himself. He had come to me in a horrible state that evening, when the company had been dismissed, to complain that the regimental-sergeant-major had called him "a miserable-looking object" (accent on the "ject"). He had taken the words very much to heart, and was quite prepared to murder the R.S.M. I had gone off at once with him to the C.O., and laid the matter before him. Honour had been satisfied, and some nasty trouble averted. Still, I was afraid my sergeant might not be enjoying himself at the festive board. My fears, however, were entirely dispelled when I heard him declaring to the old farmer: "*Alleyman no bon, Francy bon, Francy vin* (to rhyme with our word "fin") *bahut bon!*" The old soldiers often eked out their French with Hindustani.

We remained two days at Pissy. The *padre* said Mass on one of the mornings in the chapel of the fine *château* of *Madame la Marquise* (where our Battalion Headquarters were installed), *Madame* was a very beautiful invalid. A row of pale, fair-haired children knelt beside her, with their governess. *Monsieur le Marquis* was away with his regiment.

From Pissy we marched along a splendid "*Route Nationale*" to the little village of Courcelles, where we were to remain for three weeks. The delay affected the whole division, and it was to be a pleasant delay for us.

We arrived at Courcelles in the beginning of November, 1915. We left it for Marseilles in the last week of that month. It was a pretty little village of the feudal type, growing up under the aegis of its *château*. This is not to say that the latter was feudal. On the contrary, it was nothing but a fine, modern country-house. But the village owed its existence, I imagine, entirely to the *château*.

To get to the village you turned off at right-angles from the high-road, descended abruptly into a narrow valley, and then climbed up the other side. Its full name was Courcelles-sous-Moyencourt. The *château* became our Headquarters, and practically all the officers of the battalion were lodged in it. It belonged to the Marquis de Saint B——. He was in a *Chasseur* regiment, and had lately been severely wounded. *Madame* was with him in Paris. Their two boys and a girl were home for their Christmas holidays from school, but they lived in a smaller house in the grounds. The house was in reality shut up, but its owner had very hospitably thrown it open for our reception.

Never was there a more complete and welcome change than from the discomfort and danger of the trenches and close-up billets to the luxury and perfect security of our new abode. For the first time in France all the officers of the battalion were able to dine together in mess—the dining-room of the *château* being used for this purpose. There was a billiard-room, well-appointed, and containing some fine sporting books and prints. All the bedrooms were placed at our disposal, and I had a cosy one to myself. The evenings were long, and it was a delight to sit in one's room over a log-fire, reading in a comfortable armchair. The wind used to whistle outside and, in the chimney, but it was snug and warm within.

By some chance the outer door of my room acted as an aeolian harp, and weird and beautiful music used to sound all night, as the wind raced down the passages of the great house. At the top of the stairs there was a large polished hall, with a screened-off oratory. A pair of remarkably fine Siberian wolves, well-set up, stood sentinel in this upper hall, and boars' heads and other trophies of the chase covered the walls. The principal bedrooms opened on to this hall.

We were out-of-doors most of the day, although there was a good deal of rain. Our men were well housed, some in the large *manège* which stood in the grounds, others in granaries in the village. The *château* domain was extensive and very well laid out. There were ornamental ponds and some fine groups of hunting statuary, and much fine timber, beneath which were sylvan summer-houses and cunningly-constructed grottoes. Beyond the domain the land was all either heavily cultivated or preserved. To do our drill and exercises we used generally to go beyond the Amiens road, where there was plenty of room to manoeuvre; but we also did a good deal in the way of outpost training, etc., just outside the walls of the domain.

We carried out a sort of intensive training in "open warfare," the idea being that that was what we had to look forward to in "Serbia." The men (and young officers) needed this training badly, most of them never having had experience of anything beyond trench work. Fortunately, there were a few N.C.O.'s of the old order left with the Battalion, and the help which these rendered was very valuable. The training was diversified by long route-marches, mostly along the *Route Nationale*, either in the direction of Poix or in that of Quevauvillers.

The ground was indeed admirably suited for training in every kind of warfare. I even discovered a gorge in which we were able to practise "crowning the heights," an exercise in which I had been well grounded in Northern India, and which was bound to be of great importance in the country to which we were going. Classes were also started in

170

visual signalling and scouting, and we had our first demonstration (as a return to trench warfare) of the new method of "bombing along trenches."

It snowed heavily for a few days, and on one occasion I took my men for a wonderful march in a great State-owned wood that was full of deer and wild-pig. We came, I remember, to a clearing where there was a steep slope into a little valley full of soft snow. How everybody enjoyed sliding down that slope! On one of those days an orderly arrived with a message to the effect that my company sergeant-major was to go at once to Brigade Headquarters for an interview with the general. I had recommended him for a commission, and this interview was a preliminary to his getting it. Very proudly, and yet shyly, he went off down the road, in full view of all the men.

On Sundays and big festivals, we used to assemble for Mass in the village church, which we would fill completely. A buxom lass (much admired by our N.C.O.'s) used to take round the plate, with results that must have been gratifying to the finances of the little parish. The children of the *château* used to occupy the family pew in front, while the officers knelt immediately behind them. Then came the N.C.O.'s and men, filling the body of the church and overflowing into the choir-loft and beyond the door. A beadle (or *Suisse*) used to attend in semi-state, having left his hat and sword in the vestry.

The unaffected piety of our men in church always produced a most favourable impression on the French. One had always felt what a priceless asset their religion would prove to them in war. As a matter of fact, experience proved that it was almost everything to them. Outsiders marvelled at the store which they set upon the ministrations of the priest; but we of the regiment knew.

My birthday occurred while we were at Courcelles, and I and a few choice friends went into Amiens to celebrate it.

The nights were bitterly cold now, and it was good to ensconce oneself in one's room, in front of a fire. I read Renan's *Souvenirs de la Jeunesse*, and other works which I found on the shelves. In the billiard-room was a game-book, containing the records of many a happy *parti de chasse* of pre-war days, and the perusal of this brought back memories of great days at home. I look back to those three weeks which we spent at Courcelles-sous-Moyencourt as being among the pleasantest of the war. In spite of the prohibition which existed in France against the shooting of game in wartime, I managed to wheedle a 16-bore gun and cartridges out of the caretaker, and another officer and I used to go out together of an afternoon on horseback and bag a few hares and partridges. We used to take it in turns to shoot, while the one who was not shooting held the ponies. We were even making arrangements for a pig-stick, when our marching orders came.

About the last week in November we set out by road for Pissy, where we slept the night, and next day we marched to a station outside Amiens at which we entrained for Marseilles.

The train journey to Marseilles took about three days. It was pleasant enough, sauntering along through that incomparable land of the Midi. It was dark when at length we arrived at Marseilles and marched through the town and out to the rest-camp. There we were accommodated in tents, but I and a few friends got back late that night into Marseilles, and had a sumptuous dinner at a restaurant. We drank a wine which we christened "Liquid Sunshine."

The following morning, I climbed with G—— to the pine-clad ridge that overlooks the camp and harbour, on the one side, and the open sea upon the other. The warm Mediterranean sun drew incense from the trees and pine-needles. The sky was blue overhead with a blue that was a piece of heaven, and the sea reflected it joyously from beyond the rim of dazzling sand. It was indeed good to be alive!

Suddenly, while yet we gazed, down below us in the camp a bugle sounded the "Fall in!" We scrambled quickly down the slope, and took our places.

Our embarkation orders had arrived.